CONTEMPO
CHINA

MW00986901

THE COMMUNIST PARTY OF CHINA AND CONTEMPORARY CHINA

By Yang Deshan & Zhao Shumei

 China Intercontinental Press

图书在版编目（ＣＩＰ）数据

中国共产党与当代中国：英文 / 杨德山，赵淑梅著；朱建廷，肖颖译 . -- 北京：五洲传播出版社 , 2014.6（当代中国系列 / 武力主编）

ISBN 978-7-5085-2788-8

Ⅰ . ①中… Ⅱ . ①杨… ②赵… ③朱… ④肖… Ⅲ . ①中国共产党－党的建设－英文②社会发展－中国－英文 Ⅳ . ① D26 ② D668

中国版本图书馆 CIP 数据核字 (2014) 第 124442 号

- -

当代中国系列丛书

主　　编：武　力
出 版 人：荆孝敏
统　　筹：付　平

中国共产党与当代中国

著　　者：杨德山　赵淑梅
译　　者：朱建廷　肖　颖
责 任 编 辑：王　峰
图 片 提 供：中新社　CFP　东方 IC　FOTOE
装 帧 设 计：丰饶文化传播有限责任公司
出 版 发 行：五洲传播出版社
地　　址：北京市海淀区北三环中路 31 号生产力大楼 B 座 7 层
邮　　编：100088
电　　话：010-82005927，82007837
网　　址：www.cicc.org.cn
承 印 者：中煤涿州制图印刷厂北京分厂
版　　次：2014 年 6 月第 1 版第 1 次印刷
开　　本：787×1092mm 1/16
印　　张：13.25
字　　数：180 千字
定　　价：108.00 元

Contents

Preface

As a Marxist political party in China, the Communist Party of China has experienced extraordinary courses for more than 90 years since its establishment in 1921. Along with its rapid enhancement in the national strength and the growing international influence, the People's Republic of China is attracting more and more attention from the international community. It has even become a dazzling rising star among the family of nations. As such, the governing Communist Party of China has naturally become a target to be known by more and more people. This book hopes to shoulder such a responsibility and uses a popular and easy-to-understand language to give a relatively complete introduction to the contemporary Communist Party of China to the readers.

First of all, we will get back to the process of contemporary China and summarize the scientific judgments of the Communist Party of China on the world and domestic conditions at different times. In this way, we will show the historical vision of the great rejuvenation of the Chinese nation towards which the Communist Party leads the whole nation to strive forward, and inspect the

Party's key role in pressing ahead the progress of various sectors of economy, politics, culture, society and ecology in China.

Next, we cast our focus to the Communist Party of China itself and try to understand its organizational structure and answer the following questions. As the world's No.1 political Party with more than 80 million members, how does the Communist Party of China admit new members and choose and promote its cadres? How many levels is the organizational system of the Communist Party of China divided? What are the relations between each level? By which organizational principle does the Communist Party of China operate? Compared with other political parties and organizations, what features does the organization of the Communist Party of China have?

Once again, we will place the Communist Party of China in the capacity of a ruling party to inspect its interactive situations with various elements of politics and society of China, learn how it leads its legislative organizations, government, patriotic united front and social communities to mobilize various social resources to serve governance goal at different times. At the same time, we will introduce the core of governance philosophy of the Communist Party of China and its continuous scientific ways of governance.

In the end, the Communist Party of China is not a changeless, ossified and stubborn political party. It has always been paying attention to its own construction ever since its establishment, particularly after it became a ruling Party, so as to continuously adapt to the new requirements set by the new situation at home and abroad. This is the important reason why the Communist Party of China is able to be in power for long terms and gain outstanding governing achievements. We will introduce the readers the main contents and core measures of the self-construction of the Communist Party of China and its results and future development.

In the length of between 70,000 and 80,000 words, it is not easy to introduce the Communist Party of China in an objective, justified, dimensional and dynamic way. Adding to the limitations of the knowledge and time, this book should have many unsatisfied elements. Besides, this book aims to serve as a modest spur to induce more valuable opinions. Generous criticisms from readers are welcome.

The Communist Party of China and Contemporary China

In the course of China's recent political evolution since 1840, advanced personages from different classes and strata had striven to explore ways to realize China's independence and prosperity, but ended with failure due to various reasons. China hadn't showed a brand new look until Chinese proletariat and the CPC ascended the arena of history. In 1949, the CPC replaced the Kuomintang and became the ruling party of China. Since then, the CPC's long-term ruling in China has been an important part and embodiment of the political system with Chinese characteristics. The economic development, political progress, cultural flourish, social prosperity, ecological improvement and all achievements of modern China are all closely tied with the efforts of CPC.

Make Scientific Judgment on World Situation and National Conditions, Strive for National Rejuvenation

In his opening address at the 1st Plenary Meeting of the CPPCC held in 1949, Mao Zedong affectionately uttered the now famous words: "Dear delegates, we all have the common feeling, that is, our work will be recorded in human being's history and indicate that the Chinese who account for one-fourth the world's humanity have stood up." During the 60 years after that, the CPC has been engaged in leading all Chinese people to achieve the great rejuvenation of the Chinese nation and exploring effective ways to realize the noble ambition under changing domestic and international situation.

On September 21, 1949, Mao Zedong delivers an opening speech at the 1st Plenary Session of the CPPCC.

To respond to the Cold War, on one hand, the CPC has insisted on Peaceful Diplomacy to make friends worldwide and unremitting efforts in boosting world peace and humankind progress. On the other hand, the CPC has struggled with and won victories over powerful enemies to safeguard the territorial sovereignty and national core benefits, and improved its international reputation. From then on, Chinese people have started to independently explore the road toward national prosperity. However, for a rather long period, some leaders of the CPC had believed that the World War III would take place sooner or later and the socialism would gain new development after the war based on historical experience. Thus, a great deal of human and material resources was invested to cope with the possible war threat, which restricted the country's development and national rejuvenation to a great degree.

With the change of world situation, especially the fundamental adjustment of relationships between China and the U.S., and between China and Japan, the CPC had gradually changed the previous views and strived to delay the occurrence of a world war for more time in economic development. Then, the CPC made the following judgment: "Peace and development are the two outstanding issues in the world today." In March 1985, in his conversation with a foreign friend, Deng Xiaoping said the Party and government's new views to global situation, "although there is still the danger of war, the forces that can deter it are growing, and we find that encouraging." "The two really great issues confronting the world today, issues of global strategic significance, are: first, peace, and second, economic development. The first involves East-West relations, while the second involves North-South relations. In short, countries in the East, West, North and South are all involved, but the North-South relations are the key question." When the Cold War ended, the CPC still insists on Deng's judgment on world situation in 1980s. In September 1997, in the 15th CPC Congress, Jiang Zemin emphasized, "international situation moves toward relaxation in general, and peace and development are the two outstanding issues in the world today." After entering the 21st century, the CPC continued the view. In November

2012, at the 18th CPC Congress, Hu Jintao pointed out once again, "the world is experiencing profound and complicated changes, but peace and development are still the themes of the times." Of course, over the past thirty years, the CPC has never desolated precaution against forces jeopardizing world peace and believed that the more prosperous China is, the more peaceful the world will be. The judgment or recognition to the world situation offers basis for carving the road toward and defining the steps for the rejuvenation of Chinese nation at the new period.

While making scientific judgment to international situation, the CPC's recognition to the fundamental realities of the country to realize national

In April 1974, Deng Xiaoping led the Delegation of China to attend the 6th Special Session of the UN General Assembly. In the picture Deng is elaborating the principles of China on foreign relations.

rejuvenation has been continuously deepened. The core thought is expressed in the theory on "the primary stage of socialism." In the report at the 13th CPC Congress in 1987, our Party has already made a clear and definite statement on this question: "China is now in the primary stage of socialism." There are two aspects to this thesis. "First, the Chinese society is already a socialist society. We must persevere in socialism and never deviate from it. Second, China's socialist society is still in its primary stage. We must proceed from this reality and not jump over this stage." The development stage is: "It needs at least 100 years from the completion of socialist transformation to private ownership of means of production in 1950s to the realization of socialist modernization. The whole period belongs to the primary stage of socialism." The development trend is: we shall gradually put an end to poverty and backwardness. It is a stage in which an agricultural country, where farming is based on manual labour and where people engaged in agriculture constitute the majority of the population, will gradually turn into a modern industrial country where non-agricultural workers constitute the majority. It is a stage in which a society with the natural and semi-natural economy making up a very large proportion of the whole will turn into one with a highly developed commodity economy. It is a stage in which, by introducing reforms and exploring new ways, we shall establish and develop socialist economic, political and cultural structures that are full of vitality. Lastly, it is a stage in which the people of the whole country will rise to meet the challenge and bring about a great rejuvenation of the Chinese nation. The basic line of the Communist Party of China in the primary stage of socialism is to lead the people of all ethnic groups in a concerted, self-reliant and pioneering effort to turn China into a prosperous, strong, democratic and culturally advanced modern socialist country by making economic development the central task while upholding the Four Cardinal Principles and the reform and opening up policy. Since then, in the reports of the CPC congresses, the basic characteristics of the primary stage have been summarized to define the development goals of the Party and the country in the upcoming five or ten years. The views on "socialist primary stage" not only enrich the theory of scientific socialism but also emancipate the thought of Chinese people and enable them to strive more steadfastly.

Over the past three decades, China has maintained a rapid economic growth, two times higher than the world's average growth rate of 3% for the same period. Even under the pinch of international financial crisis in 2009, China still maintains an economic growth of 8.7%. Now China's economic aggregate accounts for 6% of the world's total, ranking No. 2 in the world. On November 29, 2012, when visiting the Road of Rejuvenation exhibition in Beijing, Xi Jinping said: Everyone is talking about Chinese dream. In my opinion, to realize the great rejuvenation of Chinese nation is the greatest dream of the nation. On March 17, 2013, at the closing meeting of the 1st Session of the 12th NPC, Xi

From October 25 to November 1, 1987, the 13th National Congress of the CPC was held in Beijing. The *Report on Taking the Socialist Road with Chinese Characteristics* was approved. The report gave systematic explanation about the theory of "primary stage of socialism" based on the thoughts of Deng Xiaoping. The picture shows the venue of the 13th National Congress of the CPC.

On September 25, 2009, the exhibition themed on *The Road to Revive* was held in Beijing, as a permanent exhibition at the National Museum. In the picture the visitors are watching the pictures of the attendees to the 1st National Congress of the CPC.

further expounded Chinese Dream. He said, "to realize the Chinese Dream of the great rejuvenation of Chinese nation is to realize the prosperity of the country, the rejuvenation of the nation and the happiness of the people, which both embodies the ideal of contemporary Chinese people and reflects our ancestors' glorious tradition of unremitting pursuance for progress." Nowadays, China is advancing toward the great rejuvenation of Chinese nation under the leadership of the CPC.

Lead Modernization Construction, Enhance People's Living Standard

In the march to boost the great rejuvenation of the Chinese nation, the CPC has been focusing on improving the people's living standard. After the founding of new China, the CPC had concentrated on recovering national economy, and three years later, seen over 30% increase in per peasant household actual earnings and 70% increase in urban employees' wages comparing to those in 1949. Thus, the CPC established the new democratic economic order and initiated the 1st Five-Year Plan in 1953 to lead the country to stride toward industrialization.

When the socialist basic economic system was established in 1956, the CPC started to explore the modernization road for the country under the new system. While reading the *Political Economy Textbook* of the Soviet Union from the end of 1959 to early 1960, Mao Zedong noted, "developing socialism requires modernizations in industry, agriculture, science and culture, and I'll

Li Fuchun, vice premier of the State Council and director of the State Planning Commission, is making the report on the first Five-Year Plan for the development of the national economy at the 12th Session of the 1st National People's Congress.

add the modernization in national defense." This is the initiation of the complete and far-reaching slogan "realizing the four modernizations of socialism." At the 1st session of the 3rd NPC in December 1964, in the *Report on the Work of the Government*, Zhou Enlai, based on Mao's suggestion, firstly set forth: within the 20th century, building China into a powerful socialist country with modern agriculture, industry, national defense and science and technology; and defining the two-step design for realizing the Four Modernizations: first, within 15 years, building an independent and relatively complete industrial system and national economy system to bring Chinese industry close to the global advanced level in general; second, striving to bring Chinese industry to the global leading group and completely realizing modernizations in agriculture, industry, national defense and science and technology.

But one and a half years after setting forth the aim, the Cultural Revolution broke out and completely disturbed the initial plan. However, a group of old cadres with Zhou Enlai and Deng Xiaoping as the representatives had insisted on the Four Modernizations all along. At the 1st Session of the 4th NPC held in January 1975, despite of the incurable disease, Zhou Enlai restated the Four Modernizations in the Report on the Work of the Government and deployed the future work: we shall fulfill or outperform the 4th Five-year Plan in 1975, and then we shall lay a more stable foundation for realizing the said first-step design before 1980. As for domestic and international situation, the upcoming ten years will be a key decade for realizing the said two-step strategy. Then, during the period when Deng Xiaoping presided over the work of the CPC Central Committee and the State Council, in order to realize the Four Modernization, despite of the severe environment, he proposed the goals of "promoting stability and unity" and "improving national economy to a high level" and bravely drove a complete reform, which greatly improved Chinese economy and achieved gross output value of industry and agriculture of 450.4 billion yuan in 1975, a year-on-year growth of 10.7%.

The 3rd Plenary Session of the 11th CPC Congress in 1978 gradually took the progress and development of modern China back to modernization and rejuvenation of China. In June 1981, the "Resolution on Certain Questions in the History of Our Party since the Founding of the People's Republic of China" adopted at the 6th Plenary Session of the 11th CPC Congress pointed out: "In socialist construction, we must proceed from China's specific conditions, do according to our abilities, strive actively and realize modernization goals by stages." In April, 1984, in a talk with the British Foreign Secretary Geoffrey Howe, Deng Xiaoping assumed the development aim after being a moderately prosperous society, "Our first goal is to realize a comparatively prosperous society by the turn of the century, and the second goal is to achieve or approach the living level of developed countries within another 30 to 50 years." In April, 1987, when meeting with Alfonso Guerra, vice-premier of Spain, Deng first proposed the "three-step strategy": Our goal for the first step is to reach, by 1990, a per capita GNP of US$500. That is, double the 1980 figure of $250. The goal for the second step is, by the turn of the century, to reach a per capita GNP of $1,000. When we reach that goal, China will have shaken off poverty and achieved comparative prosperity. When the total GNP exceeds $1 trillion, the national strength will increase considerably, although per capita GNP will still be very low. The goal we have set for the third step is the most important one: quadrupling the $1 trillion figure of the year 2000 within another 30 to 50 years. That will mean a per capita GNP of roughly $4,000 — in other words, a medium standard of living."

Under the leadership of the CPC, with the joint efforts of all Chinese people, we achieved the goal of "double the 1980 figure" for the first step in 1987, three year ahead of schedule. In 1995, we quadrupled GNP five years ahead of the schedule. In 1997, we quadrupled the per capita GNP ahead of the schedule. By 2000, the first and second steps of the Three-Step strategy were successfully realized. The people started to live a comparatively prosperous life. On the eve of the 21st century, the 15th CPC Congress confidently sketched a "new three-

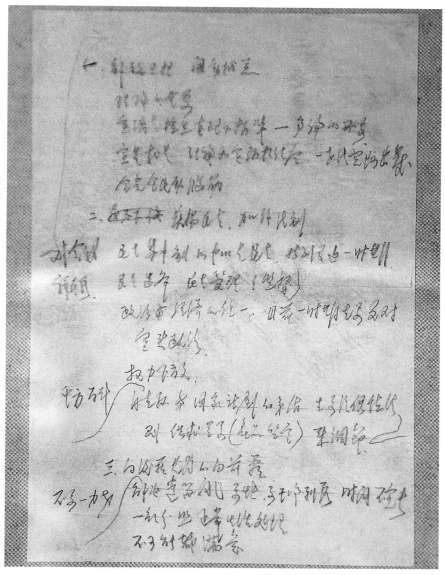

Photo of the manuscript of the speech outline written by Deng Xiaoping before the central working conference on December 13, 1978. Deng delivered a speech titled *Emancipate the Mind, Be Practical and Realistic and Look forward Corporately* at the conference. The speech was actually the keynote report at the Third Plenary Session of the 11th National Congress of the CPC held later.

stage" strategic goal: In the first decade, the gross national product will double that of the year 2000, the people will enjoy an even more comfortable life and a more or less ideal socialist market economy will have come into being. With the efforts to be made in another decade when the Party celebrates its centenary, the national economy will be more developed and the various systems will be further improved. By the middle of the next century when the People's Republic celebrates its centenary, the modernization program will have been accomplished by and large and China will have become a prosperous, strong, democratic and culturally advanced socialist country. In November 2002, the 15th CPC Congress put forward the goals for the first two decades in the 21st century: We need to concentrate on building a well-off society of a higher standard in an all-round way to the benefit of well over one billion people in this period. We will further develop the economy, improve democracy, advance science and education, enrich culture, foster social harmony and upgrade the texture of life for the people. The two decades of development will serve as an inevitable connecting link for attaining the third-step strategic objectives for our modernization drive as well as a key stage for improving the socialist market economy and opening wider to the outside world. Building on what is achieved at this stage and continuing to work for several more decades, we will have in the main accomplished the

China's Three-Step Development Strategy

The First Step:	In 1981−1990, double the 1980's GNP figure to solve the people's food and clothing problems.
The Second Step:	In 1991−1999, double the 1990's GNP figure and achieve comparative prosperity.
The Third Step:	By the mid-21st century, achieve a per capita GNP of a medium standard of living and realize modernizations in general.

modernization program and turned China into a strong, prosperous, democratic and culturally advanced socialist country by the middle of this century.

After the 16th CPC Congress, the CPC has put more enthusiasm into socialist modernization and actively boosted the leap development of people's life. By 2012, the per capita disposable income of Chinese urban and rural residents had increased from less than 100 yuan and less than 50 yuan to 24,500 yuan and 7,900 yuan respectively in 1949. The food consumption expenditures of urban and rural residents accounted for 36.2% and 39.3% of total consumption, reducing 21 and 28 percentage points respectively comparing with that in 1978 when the reform was initiated. The people's life has an ultimate turn.

At the 18th CPC Congress in November 2012 and the Central Economic Work Conference at the end of the year, the CPC regarded "strengthening livelihood security, and improving people's living level" as an important work. So in an upcoming period, the CPC will be engaged in further improving the people's living level and striving to make all Chinese share the fruits of reform, opening-up and socialist modernization.

As a pioneer of the high-tech industry of China, Zhongguancun has had dramatic change since the 16th National Congress of the CPC.

Promote Political Civilization, Ensure People to Be Their Own Masters

It is the unswerving objective of struggle of the CPC to realize democracy. In 1949, the founding of the country with people as its masters indicated the fundamental changes of the people's political position. Under the leadership of the CPC, they became masters of the country and obtained the political right to manage the national affairs together. Since then the CPC has made continuous efforts to improve the political civilization to earnestly ensure the people to be their own masters.

First, the Party established the system of people's congress as China's fundamental political system. In 1954, the first *Constitution of the People's Republic of China* was adopted, stipulating the basic political rights of the people such as the equal rights, right to vote and to be voted, and political freedom such as freedom of speech, of the press, of assembly, of association, of procession and of demonstration. In the new period, the Party took great pains to improve the system of people's congress, give full play to the people's congress and its standing committee as the leading body, and exercise the power of legislation, supervision, decision-making, appointment and removal to further exert the superiority of the system of the people's congress. In the 1990s when the concept of governing the country by law was adopted, the CPC paid more attention to giving play to the role of the legal system in the state governance and social management, safeguarded the legal system, unification, dignity and authority of the country, improved the socialist legal system with Chinese characteristics, promoted legislation in a scientific and democratic way, expanded channels for the people to participate in the legislation in a proper way, enforced constraints and supervision over the power operation, urged and supported the people's congresses at all levels to exercise the power in line with the statutory authority and procedure.

Second, the Party has always stuck to improving the multi-party cooperation and political consultation system, and expanded the channels for the realization of people's democracy. In the practice of developing the socialist democracy, the Party explored two important ways to ensure the people to be their own masters: first, the people exercise the rights to vote and to be voted, or electoral democracy, which is reflected by the system of people's congress; the second is the consultative democracy which allows full consultation before making important decisions, reflected by multi-party cooperation and political consultation system. The multi-party cooperation and political consultation system and the system of people's congress complement each other and allow the democratic parties and personages without party affiliation to participate in the management of state and social affairs, and play an important role in the social

On People's Democratic Dictatorship, by Mao Zedong, published on June 30, 1949 to celebrate the 28th anniversary of the founding of the CPC.

and state affairs management, political consultation, democratic supervision and safeguarding social stability, allow full expression of the political appeals of different classes and different social groups within the political system so as to mobilize all the positive forces to the largest extent and ensure the realization of the people's democracy.

Third, to ensure the equality, solidarity, mutual-assistance and common prosperity of all ethnic groups, the Party has explored and formed the system of regional ethnic autonomy within the unified multi-ethnic country. In the early days when New China was founded, many things were being waited to be done and the issue of ethnic works was put on the top agenda of the Party and the central government. On the basis of sticking to the basic policies of ethnic equality, unity and common prosperity, the Party has exercised democratic reform in the area of ethnic groups and set up the socialist system to free the ethnic groups from the old one. Meanwhile, with full respect to the will of the ethnic groups, the Party has exercised the ethnic autonomy system in the area where the ethnic groups inhabit to allow the ethnic groups to manage their own

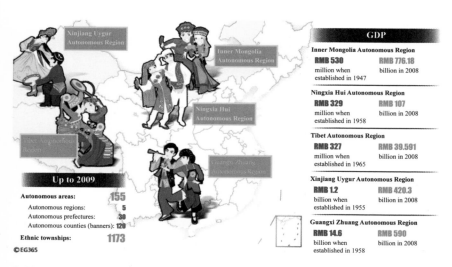

Achievements made by China in regional autonomy of ethnic groups.

affairs. In this way, the equal political rights of ethnic groups are protected. In the new period, the Party was dedicated to implementing and safeguarding the autonomy system in the ethnic areas with legislation. In May 1984, the 2nd Plenary Session of the 6th National Congress of the CPC adopted the *Law of the People's Republic of China on Regional Ethnic Autonomy* and realized the integration of policies, system and laws. From the year of 2001 when amendment was made to the *Law on Regional Ethnic Autonomy* according to the actual situation of the socialist market economy to the year of 2005 when the *Several Provisions of the State Council on Implementing the Law on Regional Ethnic Autonomy* was promulgated, China has gradually formed a national law and regulation system, including the *Constitution*, basic laws, other laws, administrative regulations, departmental provisions, regional regulations and government orders. With improved regional ethnic autonomy system, the ethnic groups of China administrate affairs of their own ethnic group and their regions, formulate autonomy provisions and orders, independently arrange and manage the economic development and develop cultural and social causes. Consequently, the economic and social situation has significantly improved.

On September 1, 2005, the square of the Potala Palace was covered by colored flames to celebrate the 40th anniversary of the Tibet Autonomous Region.

Finally, the Party has made active efforts to promote the fundamental program of democratic autonomy at the primary level of society, improving the sense of participation, awareness of rights and independent consciousness of the masses. In the new period of the implementation of the reform and opening up policy, the Party regarded to meet the requirements of the masses on democracy and mobilize their enthusiasm as the basic driving force of reform and opening up and gradually set up the primary self-governance system. That means the urban and rural residents, based on the relevant laws, regulations and policies, directly exercise the democratic election, democratic decision-making, democratic management and democratic supervision and other rights, self-management, self-service, self-education and self-supervision under the leadership of the primary Party organizations in the residential area. Specifically, the rural area has adopted the system of villagers' meeting or villager representative meeting, designed the villager self-governance rules or the village rules, set up the democratic financial management, financial audit, village affair management and other systems, and developed effective ways for election based on direct recommendation and election on the basis of two recommendations to ensure the democratic rights of farmers. In the urban area, the residential committee system was adopted in the 1980s and in the 21st century, the system was gradually changed to the community resident self-governance system. At present, the self-governance system is popularized from the large cities to the medium and small cities, from eastern China to western China with efforts to improve the urban resident self-governance, set up new communities with orderly management, improved services, beautiful and harmonious environment. Consequently the democratic rights of urban residents have been fully protected. In the institutional organizations and corporations, the workers congress is exercised as the basic system to ensure that the institutional organizations and corporations exercise the democratic management system. These measures significantly promoted the democratic practice of workers in the most direct way and to the largest extent.

In January 1963, the Tibetan people in Lhasa were attending the first grassroots election.

The 17th National Congress of the CPC convened in 2007 clearly put forward, "to adhere to the path of political development under socialism with Chinese characteristics, the Party leadership, the position of the people as masters of the country, and the rule of law, and adhere to and improve the system of people's congress, the system of multiparty cooperation and political consultation under the leadership of the Party, the system of regional ethnic autonomy, and the system of self-governance at the primary level of society and promote self-improvement and development of the socialist political system." This is the first time that the Party regarded the system of self-governance at the primary level of society as the basic system of democracy and adhering to and improvement of the self-governance system as important content of adhering to the road of political development under socialism with Chinese characteristics. In fact this has systematically integrated the state-level democracy with the democratic system at the primary level of the society, facilitated democratic systems of different types and at different levels to give full play to their advantages, and their interlink and interaction, further showcased the essence of the socialist country with the people as masters of the country and allowed hundreds of millions of people to participate in the democratic system and benefit from the system.

Boost Culture Development, Enrich People's Inner World

Culture is an active reflection of certain economy and politics in ideology and has great value in promoting social progress and development. The Party has always attached importance to the cultural development and put forward the cultural outlines, objectives and policies at different stages of revolution, construction and reform according to the actual situation and the central task of the Party to improve the cultural life of the urban and rural areas, enrich the people's inner world and gradually push forward to build the socialist culture with Chinese characteristics into the era of great development and prosperity.

The amateur troupe of Zhangjiatan Village (Gulin Town, Yinzhou, Ningbo) is putting on the Yue (Shaoxing) Opera shows named *Birthday Celebration by Five Daughters* and *The Number One Scholar and the Beggar*. This fully shows the new life of the farmers in the new era and reflects the new mode of cultural innovation.

In terms of literature and art, the Party has encouraged intellectuals to make cultural innovation. In the early days of the founding of the New China, the Party put forward the cultural policies that "all flowers bloom together, all schools of thought contend" to encourage the content and form innovation and free development of various art schools. During the process, despite of many twists and turns, great achievements were made in exploring the socialist cultural development path with Chinese characteristics with the publication of a batch of popular works with high ideological, artistic, and appreciation value. In the new period of reform and opening up, not only the traditional opera, ballad, folk music and other unique artistic forms of China, best represented by the Peking Opera and Kunqu Opera, have been greatly developed, but also the foreign artistic forms such as symphony, ballet, opera and drama have rooted in China and formed the Chinese styles and schools.

With regard to the public cultural service system, the Party has formulated the objective of establishing a village- and community-based public cultural

In Hangzhou, Zhejiang, a passenger who is waiting for the bus is reading a book at the "Floating Book Booth" at the Bus Station.

service system with a reasonable structure, balanced development, sound network, effective and efficient operation and a wide coverage of both the rural and the urban areas. In the early days when the New China was founded, the public cultural service facilities were very poor. After 60 years of construction, especially in the new period of the reform and opening up, China has roughly formed a six-tier public cultural service network (state, province, city, county, township and village) with increasing input from the government in the public cultural cause and continuous efforts in promoting the cultural facility development. Meanwhile, a number of cultural programs have been carried out to benefit the people and gradually improve the public service capacity. Statistics indicate that during the *11th Five-Year Plan* period (2006-2010), the national expenditures in the cultural causes (excluding the investment in infrastructure, or administrative operation expenditures of cultural administrations) reached 122.041 billion yuan, or 2.46 times of that during the 10th Five-Year Plan period (2001-2005), a yearly increase of 19.3%. This period saw the rapidest growth since the reform and opening-up policy were implemented. The 12th Five-Year Plan (2011-2015) has made the cultural development as an important channel to improve the soft strength of China. As a result, the public cultural service system will be further improved.

In terms of the cultural industrialization, the Party has realized great changes of the cultural market and cultural industry from blank to prosperity and development. When the reform and opening-up policy was first implemented, the Party made constant efforts in innovation in the cultural theory and actively promoted the cultural system reform. As a result, the construction of cultural market system has been vigorously promoted and the cultural industry has thrived in the tide of cultural reform. At present, China has formed a unified and open cultural market system consisting of the entertainment market, performance market, audio/video market, film market, Internet cultural market and artwork market with orderly competition. A cultural oversight system was set up with comprehensive administrative enforcement of law, social supervision,

A pharmaceutical worker is showing how to cut the traditional Chinese medicine materials into slices at the 3rd Intangible Cultural Heritage Exhibition held in Xuchang, Henan.

industrial self-discipline and technical monitor as the main content. Meanwhile, the management rules of the cultural market are under constant improvement, with increasingly standardized operation. In recent years, the cultural industry developed rapidly and made increasing contributions to the economic growth. A cultural industrial structure is gradually taking shape, with public ownership playing a dominant role and different economic sectors developing side by side.

As for the cultural heritage protection and development, the Party has made satisfactory achievements. After the founding of the New China, the Chinese government, under the leadership of the Party, has attached great importance to the cultural heritage conservation and publicized six batches of key cultural heritage protection units, with 2,351 sites in total. In 2008, the third national archaeological survey was made and identified and registered more than 400,000 unmovable cultural relics. Although with a late start, China's intangible cultural heritage conservation cause has developed very rapidly and entered the advanced array of the world. Based on the *Law of the People's Republic of China on Protection of Cultural Relics* and the *Interim Measures on Identification of Cultural Relics* and other laws and regulations, the protection system of cultural heritage has been improved. China has ranked among the best in terms of the world cultural heritage nomination and protection.

In terms of the cultural exchanges, the Party has vigorously promoted the cultural exchanges with foreign countries and Hong Kong, Macao and Taiwan to increase the overseas influence of the Chinese culture. For more than 60 years, China has established good ties of cultural exchanges with more than 160 countries and regions and formed a new structure of all-round, multi-layer, wide coverage and multi-channel cultural exchanges. Meanwhile, China has set up a batch of cultural bases, culture offices or groups in 96 embassies and consulates in 82 countries. The establishment of Confucius Institute and popularity of Chinese language across the world indicate the increasing influence of Chinese culture in the international community. In recent years, the Chinese mainland attached great importance to the cultural exchanges with Hong Kong, Macao and Taiwan. The very active exchanges increased understanding and recognition of compatriots of Hong Kong, Macao and Taiwan to the Chinese culture.

On the basis of the above mentioned theories and practice, the *Decision of the CPC Central Committee on Major Issues Pertaining to Deepening Reform of the Cultural System and Promoting the Great Development and Flourishing of Socialist Culture* was adopted at the 6th Plenary Session of the 17th National Congress of the CPC in 2011, proposing the grand goals to develop a strong socialist culture in China, and requiring to realize the goals of cultural reform and development by 2020, i.e., to further promote the development of a system of core socialist values, further cultivate a fine ideological and moral atmosphere

A martial art teacher of Jiangsu University is teaching a student from Austria how to do Tai-chi Chuan (shadow boxing).

and significantly improve the qualification of our citizens; to create a greater abundance of cultural products to meet the people's needs, and produce a constant stream of outstanding cultural products; to facilitate the all-round flourishing of cultural programs, basically establish a public cultural service system that covers the whole society, and strive to equalize basic public cultural services; to make cultural industries a pillar of the national economy, significantly increase their overall strength and international competitiveness, and form an overall setup in cultural industries in which public ownership remains dominant and various forms of ownership develop side by side; to make the cultural management system and the production and operation mechanism for cultural products full of vitality and highly efficient, and further improve the situation of cultural opening up in which the national culture acts as the main part while introducing useful cultural products from abroad and bringing the Chinese culture to the world; to develop and strengthen a contingent of high-quality cultural talent, and strengthen human resource guarantee for culture to prosper and develop. In the future, the Party will lead the people to work hard to realize these goals and constantly improve the soft strength of China.

Improve Social Administration, Construct a Harmonious Society

Social management is an essential part of human society. China, as a country with fast economic and social development and a large population, shoulders extraordinary heavy tasks for social management. Since the founding of the New China, the CPC has been attaching great importance to social management. It has made long-term explorations and practice to adopt a social management system that suits the national conditions of China. In this aspect, a great number of achievements have been made and valuable experience has been accumulated. Since the beginning of the reform and opening-up, the CPC has been engaged in enhancing and improving social management in accordance with both domestic

An art exhibition given by the disabled is put on at the square of Shanghai Huaihai Park, aiming to help the disabled to achieve their self-worth and integrate themselves into the society through art cultivation and a series of activities.

and international development and changes, including making related policies and work arrangement. Emphases are laid on improving social management by changing the concepts: from the traditional "making regulation and giving order" to "focusing on providing services"; from government trying to do everything all by itself to taking advantage of all social forces; from the tradition to "put out a fire" to "source control"; from mandatory administrative measures to comprehensive management integrated with economic, administrative, moral and scientific and technical measures.

Through long-term explorations and practice, China has established a social management guiding system and a social management organization network, and has made basic laws and regulations on social management. In addition, a social management pattern with the Party committee as leadership, government officials taking charge, social forces in coordination and the public as major participants has taken initial shape. A great number of epochal and pragmatic achievements have been made in enabling floating population to be covered by urban basic public service system, showing special concerns to special groups, incubating comprehensive social organizations, building multipartite mediation work system, implementing grid management and establishing informatization platforms. This is greatly helpful for maintaining the overall social harmony and stability.

At the same time of continuously improving the social management mechanism, the CPC also pays high attention to social construction that focuses on people's livelihood to solve the most direct and realistic problems concerning the interests of the people. Before the reform and opening-up, the CPC was engaged in social construction under limited conditions. To provide better opportunities for the masses to receive education, the CPC led to reform the old education system and content. Upholding the guiding principle for school to serve the workers and farmers, it launched extensive anti-illiteracy campaign by improving primary and secondary school education and establishing a variety of cram schools. It was for the first time that the masses enjoyed equal rights for education. Under the system of planned economy, the Chinese government provided job opportunities for most of the people through unified arrangement. To a large extent, this maintained social stability. Labour insurance system was established among state-owned enterprises, while social security system was established among public institutions, and cooperative medical system was established in rural areas. Despite of low social security level and unbalanced rural and urban development, the achievements mentioned above encouraged the masses to enthusiastically devote themselves to socialist construction.

Since the reform and opening-up, especially the 16th National Congress of the CPC, based on fast and stable economic development, the CPC has been considering the need for improving people's livelihood as an important task. To fulfill the task, the first thing to do is to promote development of education. Through the hard work of more than 30 years, basic education has had a fast

Certificate of merit issued by the People's Committee of Zhuzhou (Hunan) to the people who had made great contribution to the program to eliminate illiteracy in 1956.

development, and the anti-illiteracy campaign has helped more than 100 million people learn knowledge, while the qualification of the country's people have been greatly improved; higher education has had a prosperous development, and the proportion of college students to the total population of the country has been increasing, ranking among the top array in the world. The second thing to do is to explore and establish a social security system that is adaptive to the socialist market economy system. Through continuous reform, integrated urban social security system has been established; the system of subsistence allowances has been widely put into practice in rural areas; the coverage of the social security system has been increasingly expanded, and the basic living of the people in straitened circumstances has been guaranteed, while social welfare has been improved. After the cancellation of the Unit System (unified allocation of jobs), the Chinese government has implemented a number of active employment policies and carried out a series of re-employment projects. From 2002 to 2012, more than 100 million people in urban areas were employed; the unemployment rate had been declining year by year, while more job opportunities were provided for laid-off workers and migrant rural workers. At the same time, the Chinese government has been deepening the reform of the medical and health system. By the end of June 2010, there had been 410 million urban employees and residents covered by medical insurance system, and 830 million people covered by the new rural cooperative medical system, bringing the number of the people covered by the basic medical insurance system to more than 1.2 billion, and achieving the targets set in the 11th Five-Year Plan (from 2006 to 2010) ahead of schedule while solving the problems concerning the difficulties for the ordinary people to get and afford medical services. In addition, the Chinese government has been enhancing the support to medical and health programs. The medical and sanitary conditions have been improved, and related resources have been enriched. A public health system covering both urban and rural areas has been basically established. By 2008, the total number of health organizations in China had increased to 278,000 from 3,670 in the early years of the New China, while the average life span had

At the Xiaobeigang Community, Kaifeng, Henan, the pastry cooks from Dingyuan Pastry Making Skill Training Center are teaching the laid-off and the unemployed how to make pastry.

been increased to 73 years from 35 years in the early years of the New China.

In addition to increasingly deepened practice, the CPC has been keeping its social construction concept in line with the times. At the 16th National Congress of the CPC held in 2002, it was proposed that, to build a moderately prosperous society in all aspects, great efforts should be made to accelerate economic development, further improve the democratic system, promote better development of science and education, facilitate more prosperous cultural development, build a more harmonious society and improve people's life. It was for the first time that the national congress of the CPC definitely set "building a more harmonious society" as one of its objectives, showing that the CPC had viewed social construction and social development from a new and higher perspective. In September 2004, the Fourth Plenary Session of the 16th Central Committee of the CPC adopted the *Decision of the Central Committee of the CPC on Enhancing the Governing Ability Construction of the Party*,

At the People's Hospital of Fuyang (Anhui), the farmers are applying for reimbursement at the windows for New Rural Cooperative Medical System services.

putting forward the concept of "building a harmonious socialist society", which was formally listed as one of the five major abilities that should be possessed by the CPC to achieve an all-round improvement of its governing ability. In October 2006, the Sixth Plenary Session of the 16th Central Committee of the CPC adopted the *Decision of the CPC on Several Major Issues Concerning the Building of A Harmonious Socialist Society*, which gave a systematic statement on the objectives and tasks for building a harmonious socialist society by 2020: socialist democracy and the legal system will be further improved, and the basic principle of ruling the country by law will be implemented completely, while the rights and interests of the people will be respected and guaranteed in real earnest; the trend of widened differences between urban and rural areas and between regions will be reversed step by step, and an orderly and reasonable income allocation pattern will be basically formed up, while people will have more family property and live a more prosperous life; there will be a higher rate

In 2013, the first year of the implementation of policy on trans-regional college entrance examination in Zhejiang, a total of 984 children of migrant workers from other provinces enjoyed equal treatment as that for the local students. The picture shows the students who are encouraging each other before attending the examination.

of employment, and a social security system covering both the urban and rural residents will be basically established; the basic public service system will be improved, and the management and services of governments at different levels will be improved; the ideological and ethical standards, the scientific and cultural qualities, and the health of the whole people will be enhanced notably, and good moral habits and harmonious interpersonal relationship will be further formed up; the creative vitality of the whole society will be enhanced, an innovation-oriented country will be basically established; the social management system will be improved, and a better social order will be maintained; the efficiency of using resources will be improved significantly, and ecological environment will be greatly improved; great efforts will be made to realize all-around construction of a moderately prosperous society that benefits all the Chinese people, and develop a society in which all the people do their best to get what they deserve and get on well with each other.

Based on that, the 18th National Congress of the CPC held in 2012 put forward the goals to build a harmonious society, namely to do the best to ensure that all our people enjoy their rights to education, employment, medical and old-age care, and housing, aiming to help the people live a better life. Then, a series of policies on improving people's livelihood were issued. On December 30, 2012, Beijing and Guangzhou published the measures for children of migrant population to attend school admission examinations. Therefore, great breakthroughs, shouldering the dream of about 300 million floating population and their families about equal education, were made in college entrance examination beyond household registration. So far, except for the Tibet Autonomous Region, other provinces (municipalities and autonomous regions) have all issued plans for college entrance examination beyond household registration. Although there are controversies on some details, the general tendency has been shown clearly. Since 2013, many provinces, including Heilongjiang, Gansu, Jiangsu and Guizhou, have announced their income increase plans. Some provinces have set clear objectives to enable residents' income to grow faster than that of CPI and even GDP. For example, Guangzhou set the goal for GDP growth rate in 2013 at 10%, and growth rate of urban residents' income at 11%; Gansu set the goal for GDP growth rate in 2013 at 12%, and the growth rate of urban per capita disposable income and rural per capita net income at more than 15%. By February 2013, 25 provinces had adjusted the minimum wage standard, with an average growth of 20.2%. In the same month, the income distribution system reform scheme that had been prepared and highly concerned for a long time was released. In 2012, China launched the projects to build 7.81 million affordable houses in urban areas, and basically completed 6.01 million such houses, with potential to build more than required. In February 2013, at the executive meeting of the State Council, it was proposed that, by the end of the year, the local housing guarantee

In Weifang, Shandong, the people who want to buy houses are waiting for a draw to get the chance to buy economically affordable houses.

systems of cities above prefecture level should cover eligible migrant workers in these cities.

It shows that, the CPC will be more determined to enhance social construction, while the reform will be accelerated, and the measures for the reform will be further improved. With the construction of a harmonious socialist society, better conditions for the Chinese people to live and work in peace and contentment will be created.

Preserve Natural Ecology, Build Beautiful China

The development of human civilization has experienced several stages: the primitive progress, agricultural progress and industrial progress. Currently, it is in the stage for a transition from industrial progress to ecological progress, which is a product of profound reflection of the people on the traditional civilization forms as well as a major progress in terms of the form, concept, way and mode of the development of human civilization. Ecological progress follows the basic principles for harmonious coexistence between man and nature, between the people and between man and society, positive cycle, all-around development and sustainable prosperity, aiming to establish sustainable economic development

The Shanghai Chongming Dongtan National Nature Reserve Jin Weiguo, who once lived on bird catching, has become a regular employee of the nature reserve since 2004 and is now a senior birds protector.

mode, sound and reasonable consumption mode and harmonious interpersonal relationship. It embraces that people should pursue for creation and accumulation of both material and spiritual wealth based on the objective laws for harmonious development between man, nature and society. As an important concept of human beings, it focuses on harmonious development of man and nature and promotion of ecological environment.

Since the reform and opening-up, especially after entering the 21st century, China has been paying high attention to environmental management and ecological construction at the same time of enhancing economic construction. In the middle 1990s, the 15th National Congress of the CPC put forward the strategic thought of "sustainable development", which actually has been related to the promotion of ecological progress. In 1999, Wen Jiabao, then Vice Premier of the State Council, said, "The 21st century will be a century for ecological progress." However, for a long time, many environmental protection measures were not put into practice for some reasons. It was not until the 16th National Congress of the CPC that the Party began to timely and gradually set up the new thought to promote socialist ecological progress. Therefore, ecological progress was turned from a concept to a theory, and the understanding of the CPC for building socialist civilization with Chinese characteristics was enhanced. In September 2003, Wen Jiabao delivered a speech at the National Working Conference on Forestry, making clear requirements for the development of forestry: "the guideline focusing on ecological progress should be closely followed, the overall requirements of ecological construction, safety and civilization should be fulfilled while the principles of strict protection, positive development, scientific operation and sustainable utilization should be strictly followed to carry out six major projects for the development of forestry, promote a vigorous development of social afforestation, carry out national voluntary tree planting campaign in a deep-going way and strive for a leap-forward development." The report of the 17th National Congress of the CPC in 2007 raised new requirements for the promotion of ecological progress, and set the goal of becoming a country with

The beautiful scenery of Yanfeng Dongzhai Harbour Mangrove Forest Nature Reserve, Hankou, Hainan.

good ecological environment by 2020 as one of the major goals for building a moderately prosperous society in all aspects. It was for the first time that the concept of "ecological progress" was included in the action program of the CPC. The concept has great influence on building socialism with Chinese characteristics. At the Fifth Plenary Session of the 17th National Congress of the CPC held in 2010, the requirement for "adopting the green and low-carbon development concept" was raised. Later, "green development" was written into the 12th Five-Year Plan (2011-2015) as an independent chapter, and then governments at all levels began to encourage green building, green construction, green economy, development of green mining industry, green consumption and government green procurement. It shows the determination and confidence of China in green development.

The development of concept directly promotes related practice. During the 10 years from the 17th National Congress of the CPC to the 18th National Congress of the CPC, and from the climate conference held in Bali to those held in Copenhagen and Durban, China took the lead to make and fulfill the

The cycling activity themed on "Rediscovering the Beautify of Hainan" was held in Haikou on April 26, 2014. The activity aims to promote the life concepts for green travel, civilized travel, healthy travel and accompanied travel.

commitment for green development each time. Meanwhile, from the first setting of the obligatory targets in the 11th Five-Year Plan (2006 to 2010) to the clean-up and rectification of steel and other highly energy-consuming industries, from the implementation of a number of projects for controlling sandstorm sources in Beijing and Tianjin to the issue of related energy-saving and emission-reduction plans, and from the reduction of energy consumption per unit of GDP by 12.9% to the stable operation of the mechanism for ecological compensation, China is gradually abandoning the "black development" road and turns to a "green development" road that will benefit the later generations.

To further improve the ecological progress, the report of the 18th National Congress of the CPC included an independent chapter to discuss about "ecological progress", highlighting that "promoting ecological progress is a long-term task of vital importance to the people's well-being and China's future" and the Party, the Chinese government and the Chinese people must "raise our ecological awareness to respect, accommodate to and protect nature, and must give high priority to making ecological progress and incorporate it into all aspects and the whole process of advancing economic, political, cultural, and social progress". For this, "we should remain committed to the basic state policy of conserving resources and protecting the environment as well as the principle of giving high priority to conserving resources, protecting the environment and promoting its natural restoration, and strive for green, circular and low-carbon development. We should preserve our geographical space and improve our industrial structure, way of production and way of life in the interest of conserving resources and protecting the environment. We should address the root cause of deterioration of the ecological environment so as to reverse this trend, create a sound working and living environment for the people, and contribute our share to global ecological security." For the first time, the report set a new target to "work hard to build a beautiful country, and achieve lasting and sustainable development of the Chinese nation", which aroused resonance among all sectors of society and won the support of all the Chinese people.

After the 18th National Congress of the CPC, local governments at different levels have successively made strategies for ecological development, enhanced investment in environment-related issues, such as atmospheric pollution, sewage, waste and illegal construction, and made explorations for green development and promotion of ecological progress based on local conditions. At the same time, "building a beautiful country" has become a dream of all the Chinese people, blue sky, green land and clear water have become the mutual vision and responsibility of all the Chinese people.

From believing that man can conquer nature to advocating enhanced ecological awareness to respect, accommodate to and protect nature, and then to the concept of "building a beautiful country", it shows that the governing concepts of the CPC has been gradually moved to respect the nature and the feelings of the people. Meanwhile, the spirit of the Chinese nation to be responsible for the later generations and the world is increasingly being recognized and appreciated by people in the world.

Party Member

Members are bases for the existence and development of any party. The CPC compares its members to "cells of the party". It is necessary to understand these energetic cells first to explore the reasons that the CPC can continuously drive China's development.

The Scale and Structure of the Party Member Group

When it was founded in 1921, the CPC only had more than 50 members. The CPC's early leaders proposed the principles consistent with the interests of the vast people, formulated feasible revolutionary strategy, motivated its members to carry out considerate mass work and continuously improved its reputation and achieved enormous organization development. When the People's Republic of China was founded in 1949, the headcount of the CPC hit 4.488 million, about 0.83% of the total population of China at that time. In other words, the member of CPC has rocketed by 80,000 times within less than three decades. This is an undisputable important factor for the CPC's unity with nationwide people in the democratic revolution and its final victory in the liberation war.

After coming into power, the CPC kept on improving its attractiveness and influence in social organizations and people of all strata. The headcount and percentage of the CPC members in total population have obviously improved. By 1978, the beginning of China's reform and opening-up, the headcount of the CPC members had expanded to 36.98 million, or 3.84% of China's population, sevenfold of that in 1949.

Since 1980s, the CPC has seen a stable headcount increase with an annual growth of less than 5%. By the end of 2012, the number of the CPC members had reached 85.127 million, or more than 6% of China's total population, and developed into the world's biggest party with increasing maturity.

Along with the stable growth in headcount, the CPC has continuously optimized its structure and improved its quality from the start of the new period, especially the new century, and laid a sound foundation to play its ruling role.

First, the gap between male and female and between Han and ethnic groups in the CPC members gradually narrows. When the New China was founded in 1949, the female member count was more than 530,000, only 11.9% of the total, and the ethnic group member count less than 120,000, or 2.5% of the total. In 2000, the figure of female member hit 11.199 million, or 17.4% of the total, and the ethnic group member exceeded 4 million, or 6.2% of the total. The latest statistics in 2003 indicate that, by the end of 2012, the female member headcount had exceeded 20 million, or 23.8% of the total, and the ethnic group member headcount nearly 6 million, or 6.8% of the total. In addition to the growth in headcounts, the female and ethnic group members have played a more and more important role in the Party. Among the 2,270 delegates to the 18th National Congress of the CPC in 2012, female members totaled 521, nearly 1/4, and ethnic group members 249, over 1/10 of the total.

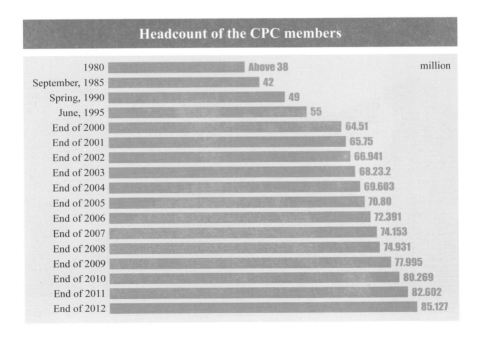

Headcount of the CPC members

		million
1980	Above 38	
September, 1985	42	
Spring, 1990	49	
June, 1995	55	
End of 2000	64.51	
End of 2001	65.75	
End of 2002	66.941	
End of 2003	68.23.2	
End of 2004	69.603	
End of 2005	70.80	
End of 2006	72.391	
End of 2007	74.153	
End of 2008	74.931	
End of 2009	77.995	
End of 2010	80.269	
End of 2011	82.602	
End of 2012	85.127	

Second, the education level of the CPC members and percentage of highly educated CPC members are greatly improved. Due to the low education popularity in the Old China, the education level of the CPC members was generally low when the New China was founded in 1949. Illiterate Party members reached 3.097 million, accounting for 69% of the total, primary school-graduated hit 1.241 million, accounting for 27.65%, junior high school and above students were at 150 thousand, only 3.34% of the total, and college and above graduates only were as low as 14 thousand, 0.3% of the total Party members. When the reform and opening-up started in 1978, the proportion of illiterate members in the total decreased to 11.9%, while the proportion of Party members with junior high school education and above increased to 41.57%, including 1.07 million members with college education and above, accounting for 2.89% of the total. In the new period, with the development of Chinese education and

On June 30, 2013, the new Party members recruited from the students of the School of Environmental and Resource Sciences of Zhejiang A&F University were attending the oath-taking ceremony.

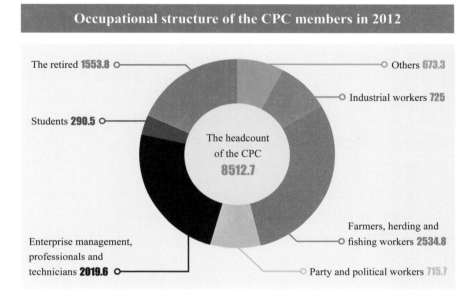

Occupational structure of the CPC members in 2012

The retired **1553.8**

Others **673.3**

Industrial workers **725**

Students **290.5**

The headcount of the CPC **8512.7**

Farmers, herding and fishing workers **2534.8**

Enterprise management, professionals and technicians **2019.6**

Party and political workers **715.7**

adjustment of policies for admitting new Party members, the overall education level of Party members, along with the proportion of highly-educated members, have seen a dramatic increase. By the end of 2000, the proportion of illiterate members had declined to 2.55% while that of members with college and above education climbed to 21.1%. By the end of 2012, more than 34 million Party members, or 40% of the total, had accepted college and above education.

Third, the vocational distribution of Party members gradually rationalizes. When the New China was founded, peasant members were dominant in the Party due to China's low industrialization, relatively low number of industrial workers and the Party's long-term growth in rural bases. After the CPC became the ruling Party, the situation was changed somehow but the members engaged in industry and agriculture were still dominant. In 1978, Party members totaled 36.981 million, consisting of workers, accounting for 18.73% of the total, peasants, accounting for 46.94%, soldiers, 6.89%, and others, 27.44% of the total. In the reform and opening-up period, with the continuous development of marketing economy, the social strata gradually diversified and the vocational distribution of Party members diversified as well. In 2012, among the 85.127 million Party members, 7.25 million were workers, 25.348 million were engaged in farming, pasturing and fishery, 7.157 million were from the Party and government organizations, 20.196 million were management and professional technicians of enterprises and institutions (including private non-enterprises), 2.905 million were students, 15.538 million were retirees and 6.733 million were engaged in other sectors.

Finally, the number of Party members from new social strata rapidly grows. Upon the entry of the 21st century, the CPC made a major change and recruited new social strata, especially entrepreneurs of non-state-owned enterprises, to be its members. According to the amendments in the 16th National Congress of the CPC in 2002, progressive members of other social strata may join the CPC.

In 2009, on the occasion of the 88th anniversary of the founding of the CPC, new Party members recruited from the staff of Beijing Hyundai Motor Company took an oath.

The so-called other social strata refer to new social strata emerged after China's reform and opening up, including founders and technicians of private sci-tech enterprises, managerial and technical staff of foreign-funded enterprises, self-employed laborers, owners of private enterprises, employees of intermediary agencies and self-employed individuals, etc. But before the 16th National Congress of the CPC in 2002, these people are not allowed to join the Party. After the congress, they became the potential targeted group of the CPC. The change is a self-adjustment of the CPC to adapt to the new situation and variation of the CPC's organization. Since 2003, the CPC has started to recruit qualified progressive people from these new social strata into the Party. During the pilot recruitment period, 226 entrepreneurs for private enterprises were recruited. When the 18th National Congress of the CPC was held, the CPC members from nationwide non-state-owned economies amounted to 2.863 million, or 3.95% of the total. In 2010 alone, a total of 131,000 people from nationwide non-state-owned economies were recruited into the CPC, accounting for 4.3% of the total recruits in the year; 83,000 people from social organizations, accounting for 2.7% of the total number recruited in the year; and 16,000 people from new social media, accounting for 0.5% of the total number recruited in the year.

Standard and Procedure for Membership

The surprising development of the CPC may produce misunderstandings, i.e. , it is easy to join the Party. But it is not. Even as an enormous team with 80 million members, each member is recruited based on scrupulous reviews at the primary organizations.

First, the CPC has rigid requirements for application qualifications. In many countries, a citizen may become a member of a party out of his/her free will without any application. For instance, in the US, voters become the members of Democratic or Republican when they vote for the candidate of either party. But to become a member of the CPC, one should be qualified in four conditions: 1) he/she should be a Chinese citizen of 18 years old or above; 2) he/she should be a pacemaker from workers, farmers, member of the armed forces, intellectuals or any advanced element of other social strata; 3) he/she should accept the Party's program and Constitution; and 4) he/she is willing to join and work actively in one of the Party organizations, carry out the Party's resolutions and pay membership dues regularly.

The CPC oath reads: It is my will to join the Communist Party of China, uphold the Party's program, observe the provisions of the Party Constitution, fulfill a Party member's duties, carry out the Party's decisions, strictly observe Party discipline, guard Party secrets, be loyal to the Party, work hard, fight for communism throughout my life, be ready at all times to sacrifice my all for the Party and the people, and never betray the Party.

Besides the said four basic requirements, to become a member of the CPC, one should display the progressiveness in consciousness and daily conducts in comparison to ordinary people. As for the awareness and consciousness, members of the CPC must "serve the people wholeheartedly, dedicate their

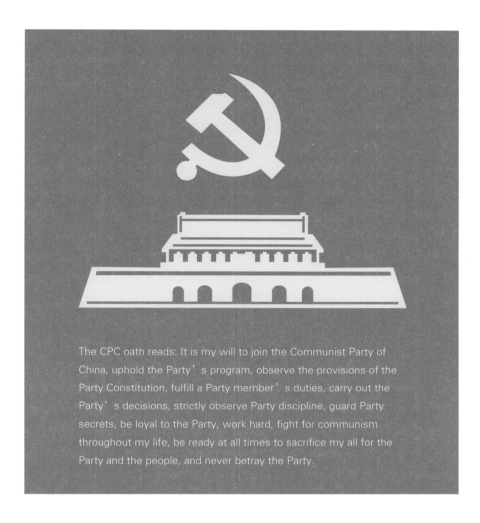

The CPC oath reads: It is my will to join the Communist Party of China, uphold the Party's program, observe the provisions of the Party Constitution, fulfill a Party member's duties, carry out the Party's decisions, strictly observe Party discipline, guard Party secrets, be loyal to the Party, work hard, fight for communism throughout my life, be ready at all times to sacrifice my all for the Party and the people, and never betray the Party.

whole lives to the realization of communism, and be ready to make any personal sacrifices." Communist Party members must not seek any personal gains or privileges, although the relevant laws and policies provide them with personal benefits and job-related functions and powers. Concerning daily conducts, the CPC members must fulfill the following duties: 1) To conscientiously study Marxism-Leninism, Mao Zedong Thought, Deng Xiaoping Theory, the important thought of Three Represents and the Scientific Outlook on Development, study the Party's line, programs, policies and resolutions, acquire essential knowledge concerning the Party, obtain general, scientific, legal and professional knowledge and work diligently to enhance their ability to serve the people. 2) To implement the Party's basic line, principles and policies, take the lead in reform, opening up and socialist modernization, encourage the people to work hard for economic development and social progress and play an exemplary and vanguard role in production, work, study and social activities. 3) To adhere to the principle that the interests of the Party and the people stand above everything else, subordinating their personal interests to the interests of the Party and the people, being the first to bear hardships and the last to enjoy comforts, working selflessly for the public interests and working to contribute more. 4) To conscientiously observe the Party discipline, abide by the laws and regulations of the state in an exemplary way, rigorously guard secrets of the Party and state, execute the Party's decisions, and accept any job and actively fulfill any task assigned them by the Party. 5) To uphold the Party's solidarity and unity, be loyal to and honest with the Party, match words with deeds, firmly oppose all factions and small-clique activities and oppose double-dealing and scheming of any kind. 6) To earnestly engage in criticism and self-criticism, boldly expose and correct shortcomings and mistakes in work and resolutely combat corruption and other negative phenomena. 7) To maintain close ties with the masses, disseminate the Party's views among them, consult with them when problems arise, keep the Party informed of their views and demands in good time and defend their legitimate interests. 8) To promote new socialist ways and customs, take the lead in putting into practice the socialist maxims of honor and disgrace, and advocate communist ethics. To step forward and fight bravely in times of difficulty or danger, daring to make any sacrifice to defend the interests of the country and the people.

Second, new Party members must be admitted through the principle of individual admission. Globally speaking, member recruitment applies to two ways: one is the individual directly joins a branch of a party, and the other is a social organization collectively joins a political party. For instance, in the

UK, nationwide and local labor unions for various industries may collectively join the Labor Party. Upon the collective action, members of the labor unions automatically become members of the Labor Party. However, the CPC thought the collective action cannot select the advanced elements of social strata and the recruits through this way have weak recognition to the Party. Hence, since its birth, the CPC has forbidden the collective action and stressed on individual's direct application for a membership.

Individual direct application for joining the CPC is only one aspect of the principle of individual admission. The principle mainly stresses on the policy of "recruiting only upon satisfying qualifications". Intensive recruitment within a short period or with lower qualifications to expand the team should be avoided. So the period that applicants wait for approvals may vary in length due to their

At the new Party member recruiting meeting of the No.2 Party Branch of the General Party Branch of Dongbei Special Steel Group Co., Ltd. , an applicant for Party membership is reading out his application for the Party membership.

different status. Thus, the overall quality of the team is guaranteed, and applicants not up to the membership requirements are urged to make active progress. Many members submitted Party Membership Application several times to request examinations by primary Party organizations. After such a rigorous examination, each member of the Party will value the membership greatly.

Third, the CPC has a strict member recruitment procedure. Qualified applicants will be defined as activists of Party application, which is the first step for obtaining the membership. At this step, primary Party branches will arrange one or two full members as tutors for the active applicant. The tutors mainly have tasks: 1) to help the activists have deeper understanding for the Party, including the basic theories, basic knowledge, basic line, member's obligations and rights etc.; 2) to examine the activist's daily performance, initiative in reporting personal ideas, work and study to the Party, attending the Party's activities, fulfilling the tasks arranged by the Party, taking part in the trainings organized by the Party and consciously accepting the Party's examination etc. In addition, the Party branch will examine the activist every six months to evaluate if he/she has a correct motivation to join the Party and plays a leading role in performance. If he/she qualifies the examination, the activist may enter the next step. Otherwise, the Party branch will issue improvement measures to help him/her make progress till his/her conformity to the qualifications. The examination is not limited to information from the tutors. Opinions from other Party members and masses will also be considered for a comprehensive and objective evaluation to the activists.

The second step is to define key objects from the activists who have accepted one-year training, and qualified the examination. These key objects will attend a 5-to-7-day intensive training on the *Constitution of the Communist Party of China, Some Norms Concerning Intra-Party Political Life.* In order to guarantee the training quality, local Party Committees invite experts and scholars from Party schools at all levels and universities to give lectures and make them have a deep understanding for the theories and rules of the CPC. After the training, each key object will have two full members as his/her recommenders who are normally the tutors or applied by the object or designated by the primary organizations. The recommenders shoulder greater responsibilities than the tutors. On one hand, they should make genuine efforts to acquaint themselves with the applicant's ideology, character, and personal experience and work performance, and explain to each applicant the Party's program and Constitution, qualifications for membership and the duties and rights of members, and make a responsible report to the Party organization on the matter. On the other hand, they should direct the applicant to fill out the Application Form and give their own opinions. Then, the Party branch committee shall strictly review the Application Form and relevant information. After being approved by the collective discussion, the Application Form shall be submitted to the conference of the Party branch, i.e. , the third step: approval and acceptance as a probationary Party member.

At the meeting for accepting probationary Party members held by the Party branch, the applicants shall report his/her understanding for the CPC, the

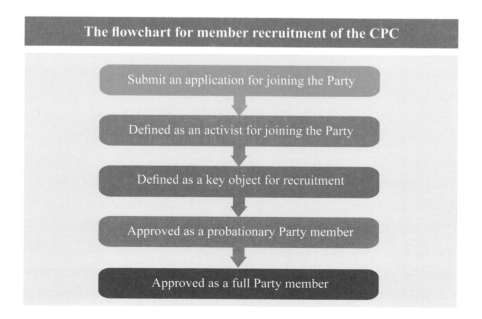

The flowchart for member recruitment of the CPC

Submit an application for joining the Party

Defined as an activist for joining the Party

Defined as a key object for recruitment

Approved as a probationary Party member

Approved as a full Party member

On February 7, 2013, the oath-taking ceremony for the new Party members of the National Badminton Team of China was held in Beijing.

motivation, personal resume and other issues need to be reported to the Party. The branch committee shall report the consideration on the applicant to the meeting. The Party members at the meeting shall make sufficient discussions on whether the applicant can be admitted and vote through raising hands or by secret ballot. Only the affirmative votes exceed half of the present full members with a right to vote, can the resolution to accepting the probationary Party member be accepted. However, the branch committee meeting have no right to approve the probationary Party member and shall submit the materials to the Party committee of the higher level who will designate a special person (Member to the Party Committee or the Party Organization Committee) to review the Application Form and relevant documents, listen to the opinions of masses inside and outside the Party, have talks with the applicant and make further investigations. Based on this, the Party committee shall make a collective discussion and vote on whether approving the applicant to be a probationary Party member or not. If approved, the upper Party committee shall inform the Party branch who will inform the applicant and declare it at the Party conference. If not approved, the upper Party committee shall inform the Party branch and the applicant with specified reasons, and encourage him/her to make further efforts and progress.

Since being approved as a probationary Party member, he/she actually has been admitted by the Party. Probationary members take part in the organization activities and work in the designated Party branch and Party group and have the same duties as full members. They enjoy the rights of full members except for those of participation in voting and elections and standing for election.

Normally, the probationary period is one year. Within the year, the Party committee will listen to the individual's reports, have conversations with individuals and organize centralized trainings to educate and observe probationary Party members. Upon the expiration of the probationary period of a probationary member, the Party branch concerned should promptly discuss whether he or she is qualified for full membership. A probationary member who is adopted at the branch meeting and approved by the upper level Party committee shall be granted full membership as scheduled. It is the last step and the final examination of the admission. If a probationary member is found not to be qualified for full membership, his or her probationary membership shall be extended or even annulled.

Last but not least, the Party also pays attention to "dredge the outlet" while "strictly controlling the inlet". For the number or the scale of a party, the quality of its members is the core element for a party's long-term development. The CPC believes that only timely removal of unqualified members can the overall quality of the team be guaranteed since there is no way to guarantee each member to make himself/herself compliant with the norms of a Party member all along, even if he/she had qualified severe examinations and admission procedures. If those who neither perform the member's duties nor qualify the member criteria are not timely eliminated from the Party, the overall impression of the people to the Party will be damaged.

On July 18, 2007, a secretary of the Party committee at town level of Xindu District of Chengdu (Sichuan) is making a work report for democratic appraisal.

After entering the new stage of reform and opening-up, in order to remove the negative influence of the "cultural revolution" and centralize the power of the whole Party into the socialist modernization cause, the 2nd Plenary Session of the 12th National Congress of the CPC held in October 1983 decided to rectify the Party. A total of 33,000 members were expelled, 90,000 were refused to be registered, and 14,000 were postponed for registration during the rectification which improved the team's quality at the critical stage of reform and opening-up. After the 13th National Congress of the CPC in 1987, the CPC Central Committee started to explore standard methods to manage unqualified Party members and formulated a series of systems and regulations. Upon the entry of the 21st century, the CPC further adheres to its basic line of keeping its advanced nature and purity. In 2010 alone, a total of 32,000 members were excluded from the Party. Most of them were expelled except that a few quitted and withdrew from the Party.

Then how does the CPC identify unqualified members? Democratic appraisement is often applied. Democratic appraisement to Party members was mentioned in *Opinions on Establishing the System for Democratic Appraisement to Party Members* issued by the Organization Department of the CPC Central Committee and approved and forward by the CPC Central Committee in December 1988. The *Opinions* requires the primary Party organizations to give objective evaluation to performance and role of each Party member in accordance with the *Constitution of the CPC* by means of positive education, self-education and mass appraisement. The basic contents shall include:

1. Whether they can firmly establish the lofty ideal on communism and the faith of socialism with Chinese characteristics, uphold the Four Cardinal Principles, consciously carry out the Party's basic route, lines and policies and keep in line with the CPC Central Committee in politics;

2. Whether they can take the lead in reform, maintaining the overall situation of reform to correctly handle the relationship among the country, collective and individuals, subordinate their personal interests to the interests of the Party and the people, and the partial interests to the overall interests, and contribute to boosting productivity and socialist spiritual civilization;

3. Whether they can carry out the Party's resolutions, strictly observe the Party's disciplines, political disciplines and the country's laws for strict enforcement of orders and prohibitions;

4. Whether they can uphold the Party's tenet, maintain close ties with the masses, help alleviate the masses' hardships, work hard selflessly for the public to consciously safeguard the masses' interest;

5. Whether they can work hard to learn professional technologies, be surefooted in their duties and strive for the first-level achievements.

After two-decade-long exploration and improvement, the democratic appraisement to Party members has been widely established across the Party. In 2012, a total of 74.282 million members attended democratic appraisement, accounting for 87.3% of the total. However, the excessive loose in evaluation standard and weak operability in the appraisement made it difficult to treat unqualified members. Hence, since 2012, the withdrawal mechanism for unqualified Party members has been successively launched for pilot operation in Guangdong, Zhejiang, Chongqing, etc. Detailed rules and regulations were developed based on the characteristics of times and the local reality to further bring the removal of unqualified Party members to standardization and institutionalization.

Education and Management of Party Members

After absorbing social elites into the Party, we strive to enable them to reach a consensus in major issues of the country and Party, form a resultant force to display the entire power. In order to achieve the target, the CPC has attached importance to the education and management to its members.

The Marxist political party attaches the greatest importance to the role of ideology, and thus emphasizes on the inner-Party education and training. During its 90-year-long evolution, especially the 60-year ruling, the CPC has explored a set of complete Party member education and training system. The education

The local government of Huoshan County of Anhui province carried out the "intra-Party warmth program" and established the Party member education and training system. The picture shows the scene that, Fang Yetao, secretary of the Party branch of Shijiahe Village of Zhufoan Town of Huoshan County, is teaching the farmers how to plant lily and prevent from pests.

contents mainly consist of the thought and political education and professional skill training. The aim of carrying out the thought and political education is to enable the Party members to apply the Marxist world outlook and methodology and continuously strengthen the recognition and loyalty to the Party's ideology. Currently, the thought and political education to the members focus on carrying out the socialist theories with Chinese characteristics and the Constitution of the CPC, and cover the basic theories, knowledge, history, lines, routes, policies and missions of the Party. The professional skill training aims to improve the self-management level and abilities in leading economic, political, social and cultural work of a member of the ruling Party. Professional skill trainings shall be offered to cater to diverse demands of Party members from different industries and positions. For instance, primary Party organizations shall offer agricultural skill trainings on scientific farming and cultivation of flowers, edible fungi and greenhouse vegetables to farmer members to make them leaders in achieving prosperity in rural areas, and offer work-related skill trainings to journalist

On July 9, 2013, Party lectures themed on "The Chinese Dream" were held at the open-type Party school at the Suihe River Park, Shuixi, Anhui. In the picture the retired Party members and cadres are listening to the lecture.

members such as writing, video editing, photography and internet public opinion evaluation to make them experts in journalism.

As for education and training methods, regular education and intensive trainings are often applied. Regular education refers to incorporating the Party member education to the routine activities of the Party organization, for instance, to learn relevant documents, discuss theoretical focuses and hold Party lectures at the periodical Party branch meeting or General Party Branch conference. Intensive trainings refer to defining specific contents, establishing special classes, holding political or technical trainings with an intensive schedule designed for the target and special at the stage. For example, in 2012, the CPC had intensive trainings covering 1.482 million secretaries from rural Party organizations, 4.353 million new members and 397,000 college-graduate village officials, and conducted trainings for Party member start-up and on employment skill for 15.233 million trainees.

During the planned economy period, both regular education and intensive trainings were a fairly great part in Party members' routine work and life. At the new stage of reform and opening-up, the CPC properly shortened the education and training time for its members in consideration of the social reality. According to the latest regulation of the General Office of CCCPC, the education and trainings to Party members in rural, urban communities and student Party members in universities shall be carried out by relevant Party committees of townships, sub-districts and schools. The education and trainings to Party members in new economic and social organizations shall be organized by the next higher Party organizations for once a year at least and above 16 hours for Party members and above 24 hours for Party construction instructors. The education and trainings for Party members in Party and political institutions, SOEs, public institutions and financial institutions shall be organized by their own Party organizations for once a year at least and above 24 hours for Party members and above 40 hours for leaders in the Party organizations.

On May 23, 2011, the Party committee of floating Party members from Suining (Sichuan) to Chengdu elected through direct election made a debut.

As for specific education and training methods, in comparison with the planned economy period and the early period of reform and opening-up, the CPC has actively explored pragmatic, flexible education and training ways to cater to new requirements of the members and received better effect since the start of the 21st century. For example, in addition to the traditional Party lectures, "mobile class" has become an important training carrier for Party member education. Party school teachers, members of lecture groups, advanced models, experts, scholars and sci-tech staff have been organized to visit rural areas, communities, enterprises and schools to help the Party members improve understandings, knowledge and abilities. Also, with the rapid development of IT and network technology, online Party schools, optional study, score management, "red" SMS and Party construction mobile newspaper have been widely applied to break restrictions of space and time, greatly improving the flexibility and attraction to Party member education and trainings. The application for new technologies dramatically narrows the gaps between rural and urban areas in Party member education and trainings and solves the imbalance of training resources to some degree. By the end of 2010, the CPC has established a modern remote education network, covering nationwide rural Party members and cadres.

In addition to the emphasis on education, training and functions of ideology, each Party member is included into the Party's management system and not allowed to dissociate the organization, which is an obvious characteristic of the CPC. With the further deepening of China's reform and opening up and the constant improvement of socialist marketing economy system, inter-industrial and trans-regional transfer and flow of people including many Party members are increasingly growing, thus a new group with "floating Party members" comes into being in the management of the CPC.

"Floating Party members" refer to those who cannot take part in the activities of the Party organizations where they belong to. In 2005, a total of 136,000 rural Party members of Anhui went to other provinces as migrant workers. In 2007, the floating Party members of Sichuan hit 239,000, accounting for 16% of the province's total. The high quantity of floating members brings

The certificate of floating party member.

great difficulty to the management of Party members, and weakens the organization and discipline of the Party. Also, some floating Party members neither take part in organization activities, nor pay the membership dues. Moreover, some of them even keep the membership record by their own.

In order to change the situation and connect floating Party members with the Party wherever they go, the nationwide floating Party member consulting service hotline (010-58586789) established by the Organization Department of CCCPC was put into operation on Feb. 13, 2007. After that, provincial, municipal and county-level Party committee's organization department successively opened floating Party member consulting hotlines. Statistics indicate that a total of 8,031 such consulting hotlines were launched for service within six months, including 3,249 by provincial, municipal and county-level Party committee's organization departments and 4,782 by the central and local departments. Thus, a nationwide floating Party member consulting service network has been set up.

In 2010, the General Office of the CCCPC issued Opinions on Strengthening and Improving Management of Floating Party Members, defining responsibilities of Party organizations for the member outflow and inflow. The

On June 16, 2011, the volunteers from the Party members of Xucun Town (Wuyuan, Jiangxi) are clearing silt for the disaster-stricken Xiaogang Village.

Party member outflow area shall educate Party members to depart, register their destination, time, address and contact information, issue certificate for Floating Party Members of the CPC, and record their thoughts, employment, life, performance and presence in Party activities. The inflow area shall undertake major responsibilities for floating Party members, including 1) carefully checking Certificate for Floating Party Members of the CPC to confirm the identity; 2) strengthening regular education and management to inflow Party members and organizing them to take part in the Party activities in a primary Party organization; 3) caring for inflow Party members and offering necessary support to their employment, study and living; 4) filling out real information on their participation of Party activities and membership dues payment in the Certificate for Floating Party Members of the CPC and timely sending their information to the outflow Party organizations; and 5) working properly in preparatory Party member's education and management. In 2012, a total of 11,000 floating Party organizations and 456,000 Party member service centers were established across the country.

However, the aim of Party member management is to urge them to be pacemakers and lead the people to build socialism with Chinese characteristics. So the Party organizations often carry out theme activities like Party Member Model Post, Party Member Zone and Party Member Reception Day to both strengthen the members' sense of honor and mission and encourage masses to supervise their conducts. Party members are also required to attend voluntary activities like poverty alleviation, education support, environmental protection, caring for next generation and donations to poverty-stricken masses to solve the specific difficulties of the masses.

In this aspect, members are the ties linking the CPC and ordinary people and the bridges between the CPC and the society for good interactions. If each member can be strict with himself/herself and play his/her roles properly, the cause he/she is engaged in will have unceasing power.

Party Cadres

For any party, there are always some backbone members who are highly motivated to promote the concepts of the party and shoulder the tasks for activity organization. Such members have different names in different parties, such as activists, active members, central members of the party, officials of the party and professional party members. In the CPC, they are called cadres of the Party.

Selection Principles and Overall Policies

Since cadres play a very important role in the CPC, what kind of person is capable of being a cadre of the Party? Since 1921, through decades of exploration, the CPC has made unique standards for selection and appointment of cadres. The Party selects its cadres on the basis of both their moral integrity and their professional competence. Moral integrity includes political loyalty, which should be evaluated based on different standards in different historical periods. During the revolutionary war period, political loyalty meant believing that communism would be certainly realized and the CPC would certainly lead the Chinese people to realize the independence and prosperous development of the

On March 15, 2011, the local government of Zhongxing Township of Guzhen County (Bengbu, Anhui) first elected the new Party committee through public recommendation and direct election. In the picture the new cadres are expressing their appreciation for the support of the other Party members.

country. After the CPC turned its role from a revolutionary party to a governing party, especially after it led China into the stage for reform and opening-up, political loyalty has been manifested by upholding the four fundamental principles, namely: adherence to socialist road, the leadership of the Communist Party, the people's democratic dictatorship and Marxism-Leninism and Mao Zedong Thought. In the 21st century, along with accelerated reform and opening-up and further development of socialist market economy, the CPC has adopted a new principle to prevent cadres from being seduced by various kinds of benefits or being swung by non-Marxism ideological trends. Such a new principle is to select cadres on the basis of both their moral integrity and their professional competence with priority given to the former. It sets loyalty to the Party and the socialist cause with Chinese characteristics as a primary factor for the Party to consider when selecting cadres. It shows that the CPC chooses competent persons with loyalty to be its cadres. It means that those only with loyalty to the Party or professional competence are not qualified to be cadres of the Party.

In addition to clear requirements for individual qualifications for being a cadre, the CPC also has definite assumption for the overall development of the cadres at different levels, namely "to make it more revolutionary, younger, better educated and more professionally competent". During the "cultural revolution", all the undertakings of China suffered setbacks. Under such circumstances, Deng Xiaoping and later leaders of the CPC believed that one of the key measures for avoiding further big turbulence is to select the "successors" in an appropriate way. For this purpose, the core task is to make the cadres at different levels more revolutionary, younger, better educated and more professionally competent. The CPC believes that, to meet the new requirements of the reform and opening-up, the cadres at all levels should be politicians who are loyal to the Marxism and socialist road and capable of governing the Party, the country and the armies, and should also be professionals who are knowledgeable and proficient in what they are working on. That is why the Party wants to make the cadres more revolutionary, better educated and more professionally competent. In this way, it

On September 8, 2012, the written examination of Beijing for selecting young cadres at department level was held at Beijing Union University.

will be able to prevent China from stepping on the capitalist road and guarantee a sustainable and stable economic and social development. To make the cadres younger is a major task based on historical experience and estimation on the development in the future. On the one hand, before the 1980s, the cadres of the Party were actually given a life-time appointment, which caused serious aging of the cadres and greatly affected the overall development of the reform and opening-up while restricting the improvement of the leading ability of the Party. That is why the Party needs a younger team of cadres who are healthy, vigorous and proficient in new knowledge. On the other hand, the CPC knows that it will take a long time and hard work of generations to realize communism. If the cadres of the Party cannot be firm to the communism, or they are not qualified to lead the socialist cause, the dream of the CPC and the Chinese people will not come true. How to guarantee continuous source of qualified successors for the Party? The key lies in cultivating highly qualified young cadres before the veteran ones retire. Based on more than 30 years' efforts, the CPC has managed to solve the problems caused by the aging of the cadres by organizing the leading groups at different levels with appropriate proportions of young and veteran cadres. Therefore, currently, the work on making the team of cadres younger is focusing more on echelon cadre cultivation and optimization of age structure within the leading groups than on making the team of cadres younger from an overall or level-by-level perspective.

Based on the principle of *selecting cadres on the basis of both their moral integrity and their professional competence with priority given to the former and the policy to make the ranks of the cadres more revolutionary, younger, better educated and more professionally competent*, the CPC has clearly defined six conditions that a qualified cadre of the Party should meet in its *Constitution of the Communist Party of China*:

1. Know Marxism-Leninism, Mao Zedong Thought and Deng Xiaoping Theory well enough to perform their duties, earnestly put the important thought of Three Represents into practice, take the lead in applying the Scientific Outlook on Development, try hard to analyze and solve practical problems with the stand, viewpoint and methods of Marxism, keep stressing study, political awareness and integrity, and be able to stand the test of all trials and tribulations.

2. Have the lofty ideal of communism and firm conviction in socialism with Chinese characteristics, firmly implement the Party's basic line, principles and policies, be determined to carry out reform and opening up, devote themselves to the cause of modernization, work hard to start undertakings in socialist construction, foster a correct view on evaluating their performances and make solid achievements that can stand the test of practice and time to the satisfaction of the people.

3. Persist in emancipating their minds, seeking truth from facts, keeping up with the times and blazing new trails in a pioneering spirit; conduct earnest investigations and studies so as to be able to integrate the Party's principles and policies with the actual conditions in their localities or departments and

work efficiently; tell the truth, do practical work, seek tangible results and oppose formalism.

4. Be fervently dedicated to the revolutionary cause and imbued with a strong sense of political responsibility, have practical experience, and be qualified for leading posts in organizational ability, general education and vocational knowledge.

5. Properly exercise the power invested in them by the people, uphold principles, handle matters according to law, be upright and clean and work diligently for the people, set an example by their own actions, work hard and live simply, maintain close ties with the masses, uphold the Party's mass line, conscientiously accept the criticism and oversight by the Party and the masses, improve their moral standards, observe the Party spirit and ethical standards, play an exemplary role, exercise self-respect, self-examination, self-caution and self-motivation, combat bureaucracy, and fight against malpractices such as abuse of power for personal gains.

6. Uphold the Party's system of democratic centralism, maintain a democratic style of work, take the overall situation into considerations, and be good at uniting and working with other comrades, including those who hold differing opinions.

The six conditions listed above show details about the cadre selection principles and overall policies, and provide extensional basis for the cadres of the Party to fulfill their duties and guarantee from the source that the cadres selected by the Party will be able to serve as a main force for the development of the socialist cause with Chinese characteristics.

Strict Selection and Reasonable Appointment

Knowing what kind of ranks of cadres should be built and how to select cadres, the core task of the CPC is to find out the way to select qualified cadres out of the huge group of Party members. In fact, political parties in all the countries in the world attach great importance to the selection of backbone members, though they have different definitions of such members and adopt different ways for the selection. For example, the British Labour Party makes clear classification of its backbone members in its Constitution, and requires

On December 28, 2010, the vote for the first public selection of leading cadres at division level of the Feng County (Shanxi) was held. In the picture 20 members of the Party committee of the county were casting votes for 12 positions.

that all the officials of the party, ranging from top leaders and assistant leaders to treasurers and auditors should be voted at the party's congress. The formal leaders of the Singapore People's Party are required to have special contributions to the party before their assumption of their positions based on recommendation of a central committee member and vote by central executive committee. Since both the Democratic Party and the Republican Party of the United States have no regular party member registration mechanism, the activists of these parties are mainly sourced from volunteers who joined in the parties on their own free will. In addition, there are many other ways taken by other parties to select backbone members, all with advantages and limitations. Considering the national conditions of China, which are different from that of Western developed countries-for example, the main activities of the CPC are not carried out based on parliamentary voting and the organization system and ranks of cadres of the Party are far larger than those of other parties, the CPC does not adopt the mode of simple democratic election, or recommendation by current leaders or use of volunteers, but adopts the mode with combined democratic election and appointment by superior authorities, incorporating the advantages of different modes for the selection of backbone members through lots of practices and explorations. Under such a mode, the cadres of the Party are selected through following four steps: nomination of candidate, investigation by organization departments, discussion and determination by Party committee, and promotion and appointment.

Nomination of candidate is made in two ways: public examination and democratic recommendation.

Public examination is an important way for the Party to select cadres, although it has just been adopted by the Party for a relatively short time beginning in the 21st century. Currently, cadres below division level are generally selected in this way. Examinations organized by Party-masses organs make up a high proportion of the national and local civil servant examinations. Meanwhile, the CPC is gradually adopting the way to select leading cadres at and above division levels through public selection. From 2005 to 2010, about 30,000 cadres were appointed through public selection, including more than 7,000 cadres above county/division level; more than 280,000 assumed office through competition, including more than 45,000 cadres above county/division level.

Considering the cost, efficiency and other factors of public selection, the organization departments may only choose to select leading cadres at and above division level through concentrated public examination under the following circumstances: concentrated selection of leading cadres is needed to improve the structure of a leading group; such selection is needed to fill many vacancies; there are no suitable candidates out of the original department for the vacancies of leadership positions; leading cadres with high professional ability and cadres in occupations that are badly needed. That's to say, usually, the organization department will not arrange a public selection for only one position.

On August 4, 2012, the interview for united and competitive selection of cadres of Ningbo (Zhejiang) was held. In the picture the applicant is communicating with the interviewers.

For a public examination, the organization department will first release relevant information about the positions, range, conditions and schedule. Applicants should be recommended by organizations or individuals and fill in the application form. The organization department will review the applications based on the conditions and qualifications as required and select candidates to attend written examination and interview. The written examination aims to test the proficiency degree of the candidates about the fundamental theories, basic knowledge, basic approaches and professional knowledge that should be mastered by the leading cadres holding the positions, especially the ability to cope with actual problems during work by using related theories, knowledge and approaches. The interview aims to test the leading ability and personality characteristics of the candidates. Integrated results of the written examination and the interview will be based on to select candidates for the observation stage. The combination of examination and observation is a result of the exploration of the CPC for selection of cadres. It enables more Party members to have opportunities to attend cadre selection, and enables cadres to be selected based on both results of examination and observation on abilities and performance in daily work.

In addition to public examination, democratic recommendation is also an important way to select candidate for a leadership position. In details, democratic recommendation can be divided into recommendation through vote at conference and recommendation through face-to-face conversation. Generally, both change of leadership and promotion of a cadre are made in the two ways, which are supplementary and verify to each other. However, different leadership positions have different requirements for the people to attend democratic recommendation conference. For example, for a change of leadership and promotion of a cadre for the leadership group, a democratic recommendation conference should be held and presided over by the organization department of the Party committee of higher level, and the attendees should include the members of related Party committee, the members or all leaders of the leading Party groups of related People's Congress, government and CPPCC committee, leading members of the commission for discipline inspection, leading members of related people's court, people's procuratorate, departments of Party committee and governments as well as people's groups, and major leading members of the Party committees or governments at the lower level. For selection of leading member for a certain department, only leading members of the department and its internal departments and units directly under it should attend the democratic recommendation conference; for department with a few members, all the members may be allowed to attend the democratic recommendation conference.

To guarantee the authenticity and the public recognition of the results of the recommendation, generally, the number of actual attendees to the democratic recommendation conference should not be less than two thirds of the number of qualified attendees to the conference. At the conference, the organization department should release the information about the positions, conditions and recommendation scope, provide name list and clarify related requirements.

On July 5, 2004, the public recommendation and public selection of Party and government officials of Xiangfan (Hubei) came to an end after more than two months. In the picture the representatives attending the democratic recommendation meeting are voting for the candidates.

The attendees should fill in the recommendation votes. The organization department will calculate the votes from people holding positions at different levels and make analysis on the prestige and recognition of each recommended person among the ordinary Party members, ordinary cadres and leading cadres. However, the CPC believes that votes may only reflect the intention of the voters for the recommended people, but cannot convey all the opinions of the voters on the recommended people. Therefore, the organization department will also arrange face-to-face conversations with people who are qualified for the recommendation to understand what they think about the recommended candidates. In this way, it may have a full understanding for the recommended people. Later, the organization department will combine the results of these two ways of recommendation and send the feedback to related Party committee as important basis for selecting candidates for observation. The Party committee concerned will not make a decision just based on the voting results. It will give sufficient consideration to the performance of the recommended people during daily work and determine the name list for observation after careful study. It will make a final decision based on communication with the organization department of the superior Party committee. The number of candidates for the observation stage should be more than the number of cadres that will be actually promoted.

Obviously, the observation is of the same significance to both public selection and democratic recommendation, aiming to make comparison of different candidates to make the best choice. It fully reflects the prudent attitude of the CPC to the selection of cadres.

During the observation stage, the organization department in charge of cadre management will form up a special observation group, which usually consists of more than two trained members. Based on the level of position and related job requirements, the observation group will make specific schemes. In order to guarantee an open and equal selection and accuracy of observation results, the information about the positions, the candidates, observation term, location and contact with the observation group will be released so that the observation group will be able to acquire information about the candidates in an all-around way under the supervision of a wide range of Party members and the masses. Specifically, an observation scheme includes face-to-face conservation, release of consultation forms, democratic appraisal, site observation, resourcing, investigation and interview. The observation focuses on the candidates' performance in morality, professional ability, diligence, achievements and integrity. Job performance should be a focus. After the observation, the observation group will inform the major leading members of related Party committee and the candidates of the result of the observation.

Following that, the Party committee will have a discussion and make the final decision, which is the third step. The Party committee attaches great importance to this process. This can be reflected by four requirements. First, the appointment of a cadre shall not be decided just by any leading member of related Party committee, including the top leader of the committee; instead, it

On December 23, 2009, permanent Party representatives are discussing about the candidates to the Party Committee at the congress of party representatives of Hongyan Township (Huarong, Sichuan) .

shall be decided through discussions at the Party committee meeting. Second, the meeting, at which cadre appointment will be decided, shall be attended by two thirds of the Party committee members, and the attendees shall promise to allocate enough time to acquire sufficient relevant information and provide their opinions. Third, based on discussions, the Party committee shall make a final decision through voice vote, vote by a show of hands or secret ballot; for candidates for principal positions of the leading groups at municipal and county levels, the final decision shall be made through the review of the plenary meeting of related Party committee and secret ballot; for a final approval, the affirmative votes shall account for more than 50%. Fourth, in case of any significant disagreement or problem during the discussion of the Party committee, the meeting shall be suspended and in-depth investigation and discussion shall be made. During the discussion, if the Party committee members believe that there is no suitable candidate for the position(s), a vacancy shall be reserved. This

On December 13, 2013, the college-graduate Party member village officials make annual assessment on the Party secretary at the Party secretary performance assessment conference at Dongxing District, Neijiang, Sichuan.

shows that the CPC has been following the principle of quality over quantity when selecting cadres of the Party.

The last step of cadre selection is the appointment. To select and promote cadres in a more scientific and effective way, the Party committee will not issue an appointment notification immediately after the final decision is made through discussion. There will be a public comment period before the appointment. The name list of the candidates to be promoted will be made public within a certain scope for public opinions. If there is no objection to the name list, the Party committee will issue the appointment notification, and the organization department will be in charge of the procedures for the candidates to assume the positions.

Compared with the methods of other parties for backbone cadre selection, the CPC adopts a mode with combined democratic recommendation and appointment by superior authorities. This mode enables the Party to follow the democratic line while listening to the opinions of all related parties. Meanwhile, it guarantees that the appointed members possess all the merits and abilities that the Party requires and that they are able to win the confidence of the Party and the satisfaction of the masses and other cadres.

There are examples that some cadres with high personal qualities were not suitable for their positions, or, they could not cooperate with the other cadres in the same group. To avoid it, the CPC has made probation a part of the cadre selection and appointment process. The probation term usually lasts for half a year or a year after the appointment notification is issued. As the probation term comes to an end, assessment will be made by the organization (personnel) department with cadre management authority. In addition to an all-around evaluation of the ideological and political performance, organization and leading ability, job performance, work style, and integrity and self-discipline of the candidates during the probation, it focuses on the adaptability of the candidates to the positions and their performance of duties. Candidates who

On August 1, 2013, Gong Qiang (middle), secretary of the party branch of Qingnan Village of Qinghu Town Comprehensive Agricultural Resources Development Project Area, was making a work report to the representatives of Party members.

pass the assessment will be formally appointed while those who fail to pass the assessment will be transferred to other positions as the case may be.

Meanwhile, to avoid a lack of motivation in work, which may cause shirking responsibilities and postponing, the CPC adopts a strict system of fixed tenures for leading positions. In details, the tenure of a leading cadre of a Party or government department is five years, after which assessment will be made again. It aims to encourage leading cadres to be highly motivated in work. To promote appropriate succession of the new cadres, leading cadres who have served two consecutive terms will not be recommended, nominated or appointed for the same position; leading cadres who have held positions at the same level (above county level) for 15 years should not serve consecutive terms for any leading positions of the same level.

Classified Management and Scientific Assessment

It is a difficult process to select suitable cadres, so is the process to manage the huge group of cadres and make everyone play an appropriate role in work. Through decades of exploration, the CPC has set up an integrated cadre management system with Chinese characteristics.

During the revolutionary war period and at the beginning of the founding of the New China, cadres of the CPC were managed by organization department in a unified way. With increasing tasks for socialist construction and increase of cadres, such management mode showed some disadvantages. In 1950s, sticking to the principle of placing cadres under Party supervision, the CPC began to adopt the following mechanism for classified management of cadres:

1. All the cadres of the Party are divided into nine categories, including cadres of armies, culture and education departments, planned industrial sectors, financial and trade departments, transportation departments, agriculture, forestry and water conservancy departments, united front departments, political and law departments, and Party-masses departments.

2. Following the example of the Communist Party of the Soviet Union, which adopts the party cadre name list system, all cadres were placed under the management of the central and local Party committees.

However, affected by the planned economy, then classified management still featured highly concentrated authority. For example, the cadres at second level were under the management of the central, provincial, municipal and autonomous region-level Party committees, while enterprises and public institutions almost had no cadre management authority. To a great extent, this impeded the economic and social development.

Entering the stage of the reform and opening-up, the CPC decided to delegate the cadre management authority by adopting the "one-level-down" management system, which features management level by level. This made primary Party committees, especially the enterprises and public institutions, more motivated, and improved the efficiency of cadre management. For the classified cadre management, the CPC changed the categories adopted during the planned economy period and gradually established a scientific classified management system fitting the characteristics of the Party and government organs, state-owned enterprises and public institutions.

For Party and government organs, the CPC established the modern civil servant system. In accordance with the *Civil Servant Law of the People's Republic of China*, the central civil servant management authority shall be in charge of comprehensive management of national civil servants; the local civil servant management authorities above county level shall be in charge of comprehensive management of civil servants within their jurisdiction; superior civil servant management authorities shall provide direction for the civil servant management of the civil servant management authorities at lower level; civil servant management authorities at all levels shall provide direction for civil servant management of organs at the same level; in the same organ, by nature of position, characteristics of position and requirements for management, civil servants are divided into several categories, including those under comprehensive management, those with professional and technical skills and those in charge of administrative enforcement. They are managed and assessed by categories. Such management mode guarantees that the public servants at different levels and in different positions will earnestly fulfill their duties.

For the state-owned enterprises, in principle, leaders of any investment institution under government authorization (including large enterprise, enterprise group, assets management company and holding company authorized to operate state-owned assets, similarly hereinafter) shall be managed by the Party committee at the same level with the government that executes the authorization.

To promote the implementation of the Civil Servant Law in 2006, the Organization Department, Publicity Department and Personnel Department of CPC Shanxi Committee jointly sponsored the "China Mobile (Shanxi) Cup" TV Quiz Show for Civil Servants. The picture is about the show broadcasted on December 19, 2005 by Shanxi Television Station.

Leaders of any enterprise owned by any such investment institution shall be managed by the investment institution. In any enterprise, the Party committee supports the board of directors to choose managers based on relevant laws and regulations, and it also supports the managers to execute their rights for arranging staff members based on relevant laws and regulations. The CPC is now gradually phasing out the administrative ranks of leaders of state-owned enterprises to establish a payment mechanism based on evaluation of profitability, social contribution, and recognition of staff members and safe production of enterprises. It is a significant exploration with full respect to the operation rules of modern corporate system on the premise of sticking to the principle of placing cadres under Party supervision.

For public institutions, the CPC mainly adopts the position management mode, which allows leaders of different types of public institutions to be employed, elected, appointed and hired through examination in accordance with specific conditions. Meanwhile, the tenure-based objective accountability system has been adopted to enhance assessment of performance of the leaders during their terms and lead them to provide good services for public undertakings. Employment system has been promoted in the public institutions in an all-around way to replace the life-long tenure system. It means that, based on relevant laws and regulations as well as the equity, free will and consensus principles, the employer and employee will sign employment contract, which will specify the liabilities, obligations and rights and interests of both parties. To further enhance scientific management, in 2012, the General Office of the CPC Central Committee issued the *Opinions on Strengthening and Improving Party Building in Reform of Public* Institutions, and proposed to speed up study and formulation of management measures and comprehensive appraisal measures for management of leaders of public institutions in different industries. In the future, the management of leaders of public institutions will be more standardized and specific.

Based on definite cadre management authority, competent management authority shall conduct regular and unscheduled assessment of the performance of the cadres on their positions. Entering the 21st century, to promote the governing concepts of "scientific development" and "people-oriented" among all the Party members, the CPC began to access the performance of cadres at different levels based on the indicators including population resources, social security, energy saving and emission reduction, environmental protection, safe production, social stability, clean and honest government and satisfaction of the masses. It plays an important guiding role for the governments and departments at different levels in fulfilling their duties. For the assessment, difference shall be allowed due to the characteristics of different regions, positions at different levels and types of cadres to enhance the pertinence of the assessment. The results of

On October 30, 2010, cadres from the Beijing government, branches of the National Library of China and ministries and commissions in Beijing attended a lecture on "Modern China: Variation between tradition and modernity".

the assessment will be used as incentive and accountability standards for cadres, and will be linked with the payment and promotion opportunities of cadres, aiming to mobilize the initiative and creativity of the cadres.

To improve cadres' operational capability and personal cultivation so that they are able to continuously meet the requirements of national and international development, competent authorities will also arrange courses and trainings for cadres. On one hand, to meet the needs of work and self-improvements, cadres at all levels should occasionally attend on-the-job trainings, which aim to improve leadership ability, update professional knowledge and keep the cadres aware of the latest development trends. On the other hand, cadres at all levels should, every year, or every three to five years, attend off-job trainings at Party schools, administration schools and cadre college for systematic learning. To ensure the effect of these trainings, competent authorities at different levels, which are in charge of education and training, and units, for which the cadres are working, should make relevant records on the courses and trainings accepted by the cadres. These records will be used as basis for annual assessment and appointment and promotion of cadres.

Training in Practice

The CPC has been attaching great importance to theoretical education of cadres. However, it also considers that training in practice should be the fundamental way to improve the abilities of leading cadres as members of the party in power. This is because: it is a good way for cadres to apply and really understand the theories and knowledge they have learnt and to improve their capabilities in actual operations; at the same time, it is only in practice can the abilities of the leading cadres for controlling overall situation and coping with complicated situations be improved through continuous self-cultivation. Therefore, the CPC attaches more importance to training cadres in practice than other parties.

Opportunities for practice are provided to cadres through the cadre exchange system. Compared with other countries, China's cadre management system with Chinese characteristics, which is based on the principle of placing cadres under Party supervision, has an advantage that allows overall arrangement and transfer of cadres to maximize the overall performance of all ranks of cadres. To this end, the cadre exchange system serves as an important carrier. It means that the Party committees (leading Party groups) at all levels and their organization (personnel) departments may transfer cadres to different positions within their authority for cadre management. During the period of democratic revolution, the Central Committee of the CPC had been aware that fixing the cadres on certain positions might cause stagnation of improvement and gaps between higher and lower levels of Party members. Therefore, it then proposed to carry out cadre exchange to a certain extent to ensure communication between the higher and lower levels, the front and the rear Party members as well as the army and the local authorities. In 1962, the Central Committee of the CPC worked out and issued the *Decision on Carrying out Exchange of Leading Cadres at All Levels in a Planned and*

In December 2003, the second group of exchange cadres from the head office of the Agricultural Bank of China to take a temporary post at Ningbo (Zhejiang) Branch visited the Beilun Port to make a survey on the development of port-centered industry.

Orderly Way, to set regular cadre exchange as a fundamental system for cadre management. However, for some reasons, the *Decision* was not put into full practice. After the 1990s, especially entering the 21st century, the cadre exchange system has been put into the track of standardized and institutionalized practice.

In addition to the prevention from bureaucracy and slow-down in work, another important target of the cadre exchange system is to cultivate and train cadres. Since the mid-1990s, the Organization Department of the CPC Central Committee has been making great efforts to promote cadre exchange in a variety of programs, including the Western Development, the programs to revitalize old industrial bases in Northeast China and other areas, the programs for the Rising of Central China, the construction of national pillar industries and key projects as well as the programs to assist Tibet and Xinjiang. Cadres are encouraged to work in less-developed areas and on the positions that need extremely hard work to promote the development of these areas and make complementary flow of the cadres. Through this process, cadres from central organs will acquire enough knowledge about the complexity of local governance; cadres of Han will understand the characteristics of the work in regions inhabited by ethnic groups; excellent and young cadres from the eastern economically developed areas will be able to bring their advanced experiences to the central and western parts of China, while excellent cadres and cadres with great development potential will get the chances to broaden their horizon and mind in the eastern developed areas. To adapt to the new governance challenges brought by the development of time, the CPC is trying to create more and more exchange opportunities for the cadres at different levels. It aims to promote the communication among different areas and departments, as well as between the higher and the lower levels of authorities, and the Party and government offices and the enterprises, public institutions and other social organizations. Meanwhile, it also aims to enable the cadres to be trained in different positions and under different circumstances, get rich experience in leadership, expand their horizons and enhance their abilities.

In October 2008, CCTV host Wang Zhi began his temporary service in Lijiang (Yunnan) as deputy mayor of the city.

The temporary service system has been established to expand channels for practice of cadres. The temporary service system is different from the cadre exchange system. It mainly aims to make up for the deficiency of experience of current cadres in grassroots work or handling the overall situation, and enable the cadres to get rich experiences and leadership ability. Therefore, cadres under the temporary service system maintain their personal connections with the original units and go back to the original units after the temporary service term expires. To a large extent, the local governments and related departments will base on their needs and cadre training plans to send some young cadres with moral integrity and their professional competence as well as great development potential to suitable areas and units through the temporary service system. In accordance with relevant regulations, the areas or units should provide necessary conditions and support for the work and living of these cadres and ensure that they may put their major efforts and time in getting in-depth understanding for actual situations and improving their organization and leadership abilities, ideology and job performance.

In recent years, with increasingly intensified understanding for the significance of training in practice, the CPC identified the needs of cadres at primary levels for opportunities to learn experience and knowledge and understand macro conditions by committing to temporary services in the positions at higher levels. With increasingly raised requirements of the CPC for the governing ability of leading cadres, adopting an overall point of view and being good at controlling the macroscopic conditions have become abilities required by the leading cadres. However, due to a lack of experience, some cadres at primary level cannot have a full understanding for the policies and guidelines made by the superiors. Therefore, it is hard to break regionalism and departmental selfishness to serve the overall benefits of the country. So far, the program has allowed some cadres at village level to commit to temporary service at stations, offices and demonstration service bases at town levels. Based on accumulated experience, it will be expanded to departments at county and township levels.

It enables the cadres at primary level to have better understanding for what the superiors do through practice. At the same time of encouraging cadres to serve the less-developed areas, channels for cadres from the less-developed areas to temporarily serve the developed areas have been established. In early 2013, a total of 536 cadres from the western part of China and other regions inhabited by ethnic groups were sent to central units and eastern developed areas to start their temporary services. Of them, there are 182 cadres at prefecture level, accounting for 34%, and 354 at county/division level, accounting for 66%.

In addition, the CPC also encourages cadres to make grassroots investigations and study. The CPC believes that, without investigations, there is no right to speak, let alone right to make decision. Therefore, cadres at all levels should make substantial investigations and study before they can make any scientific decision. The grassroots should be the foundation of the governance of the CPC, while the opinions and advice of the cadres and the masses at primary level provide first-hand information and important basis for the cadres at all levels to make decision. Therefore, cadres at all levels, from central leading

On December 31, 2009, the activity themed on "Riding a bike to the grassroots" was launched at Yuanzhou District, Yichun, Jiangxi. Cadres visited the grassroots by bike.

Cadres from offices of State Administration of Taxation made grassroots investigation and study at a timber yard in Hulun Buir, Inner Mongolia on April 29, 2007.

cadres to provincial and ministerial cadres, and then to cadres at prefecture and county levels, shall spend one to four months every year in investigations and study at the grassroots. As it is easy for some cadres to rest content with a smattering of knowledge, the CPC calls for the use of the system to allow the cadres to work at selected spots for investigation and study under certain subjects. Cadres at all levels should choose some counties, towns, villages, sub-districts, enterprises, scientific research units, schools and families as contact stations for them to get direct contact with the mass at the grassroots. In addition, for every investigation or study, the leading cadres should define clear subject according the core tasks and responsibilities of the Party committee, trying to find solutions and measures to solve the problems under the subject during the investigation or study. The vast majority of units consider experience in working at the grassroots as a qualification requirement for applying for attending the state civil service examination held every year. It is actually guiding the young people who want to become a member of the CPC to learn knowledge and experience at the grassroots first.

Organizational System

Organization is one of the basic elements of a political party. From the aspect of scale, most political parties are not a simple political organization, but a comprehensive one with concrete internal organizations. Vertically, the political party normally has the central organization, regional organization and primary organization. Horizontally, it consists of different sections classified by region, sector or function. Compared with other political parties, the Marxist political party attaches great importance to the organization building and builds a tight network of the internal organizational structure. The CPC needs to manage more than 80 million Party members, which is larger than the total population of the UK or France. However, the Party is not in a mess, but runs in order. An important reason is the establishment of a strict organizational system.

Organizational Principle

Since the modern times, every political party has its own organizational principle. The organizational principle is the thinking for the political party to integrate the basic elements of the party - its members, cadres and organizations – to make it work properly. All the political parties have their own organizational principle with differences only in the purpose, social status and members. For example, the Democrats and Republicans in the United States have committees at the national, state, county (city), and district levels and the electoral committee, but there is no administrative subordination between the national committee and the regional committees. The organizational principles of the political parties of the US allow great freedom for the local organizations at various levels and

Party members and people of Miao ethnic group of Changlai Miao Village of Rongshui Miao Autonomous County are watching the live broadcasting of the opening ceremony of the 18th National Congress of the CPC.

cause no problem in the geographical election. However, the overall strength as a governing party is very weak after the election. Another example is the Green Party which was founded in the1970s in various countries. The decision-making right of the Party is in the possession of the primary organizations, although it has the central, local and primary organizations. The upper level organizations are just the administrative body of the primary organizations. This organizational principle has a good effect in preventing the individual dictatorship in the party. However, without a unified commanding organization, the Party members who are united with the philosophy can hardly realize the purpose of governing alone as a governing party, and consequently the philosophy cannot be promoted rapidly in the whole country. In contrast with the Green Party's emphasis on the primary organization, the fascist political party emerged in Germany and Italy in the first half of the 20th century upheld the organizational principles of individual dictatorship that the leaders were paramount. Although this organizational principle made the whole party more disciplined, if the leader made a wrong order, the consequence would be disastrous. The outbreak of the World War II has fully proven the point.

Compared with the organizational principles of the other political parties, the CPC's principle of democratic centralism properly handles the relations between "democracy" and "centralization", and "freedom" and "discipline". This not only helps avoid the phenomena of loose organization and discipline caused by excessive emphasis on democracy, but also prevents the disadvantage of over centralization and individual dictatorship. The key reason why the democratic centralism can be so effective is that it not only guarantees the democratic right of common Party members and realizes the purpose of majority rule, but also prevents individual dictatorship and offers guarantee for the scientific decision-making. What's more, the principle also ensures the sense of discipline of the political party and enables all organizations at various levels to effectively and efficiently execute all decisions. Why the principle of democratic centralism can realize these three points?

First, in the intra-party authorization relations established with the principle of democratic centralism, the Party members are the main body of authorization and "masters" of the political party. In the organization of the CPC, the congresses of various levels directly or indirectly elected by Party members are the leading bodies and the committees of all levels shall be responsible for and report to the congress of the same level. This is the fundamental guarantee to the principal position of Party members. In recent years, the CPC made continuous efforts in improving the conditions for Party members to execute the right to vote. In 2004 the *Regulations on Protecting the Rights of Members of the Communist Party of China* adopted in 2004 made more detailed provisions on the right to vote of Party members on the principle that "the right to vote and to be elected is the basic right of every Party member". The Party members who take part in the election have the right to learn about information of the candidates, and request to change the candidates, elect any candidate or somebody else. In addition to the right to vote and to be elected, the Party members have the right to take part in the meetings of the Party group and the Party branches, meetings of the Party members, and meetings corresponding to his/her position or delegate qualification; the right to read documents of the Party, the right to take part in discussion about policy and theoretic issues at the Party meetings and express his/her opinions, the right to take part in discussions on the Party's policy and theoretic issues at the newspapers and journals of the Party organized by the central and local Party organizations, and the right to criticize any Party organs and members at the Party meetings. Meanwhile, the upper level organs of the Party are requested to listen to opinions of the lower level organs, members and masses and timely solve the problems they raise. The organizations of all levels must make the Party affairs public in line with the requirements to allow the members to learn more about the internal affairs and ensure their right to know. The above efforts and measures on protecting the democratic rights and the position of main body of Party members enable the CPC to really realize the purpose of "majority rule".

On May 15, 2013, the Open Day of the deputies to the People's Congress of Daxing Town of Yaohai District (Hefei, Anhui), the deputies visit the communities and the residents to listen to the opinions of the people and have face-to-face communication with the residents.

Second, the intra-party leadership and decision-making system established by the principle of democratic centralism limits the power of top leaders and main leaders and cadres of organizations at all levels and ensures the scientific decision-making of the Party. The Party forbids any forms of personality cult. Although the Party leaders are at the center of power, they do not have the absolute power, but are subject to supervision of the whole Party and all the peoples. Party committees at all levels function on the principle of combining collective leadership with individual responsibility based on division of work. The collective leadership means that all major issues related to lines, principles and policies of the Party, arrangement of important tasks, appointment, dismissal, transfer and supervision of cadres and issues related to interests of the people shall be decided upon by the Party committees, standing committees or secretariat after discussion. In the committees, secretary and members of the

On March 20, 2012, at the activity center of Yongtieyuan Community (Yongwai Street, the southern urban area of Beijing), 180 Party members got together to elect secretary, deputy secretary and members of the Party committee of the community.

committees are different only by the division of work, not under the superior-subordinate relations. Each of them has a vote in the voting. The individual responsibility based on division of work means that the specific responsibilities of each member are well defined to ensure that all affairs are undertaken and everybody has his/her own responsibilities. This leadership principle not only gives full play to democracy and limits power of the Party secretaries, but also avoids the problem that all issues are subject to the meeting discussion and the consequent low efficiency under the collective leadership.

Third, the strict discipline and regulations formed according to the principle of democratic centralism make the whole organizational system of the CPC united and solidarity and all the scientific decisions to be effectively implemented. The "centralism" in the democratic centralism system mainly refers to (1) individual Party members are subordinate to the Party organization; (2) the minority is subordinate to the majority; (3) the lower Party organizations are subordinate to the higher Party organizations; (4) and all the constituent organizations and members of the Party are subordinate to the National Congress and the Central Committee of the Party.

That "individual Party members are subordinate to the Party organization" means each and every Party member, including leaders, cadres and even top leaders, must decisively execute the decisions made by the organizations. If a Party member has a different opinion to the decision, he/she can reserve or submit the opinion to the upper level organizations. However, before the decision is changed, the Party members must execute the decision unconditionally. It is not allowed to execute the decisions which cater to their intention but refuse to execute those not.

That "the minority is subordinate to the majority" means when discussing and making decisions on any case, Party organizations must keep to the principle of subordination of the minority to the majority on the basis of full expression of

On December 13, 2013, to enhance security monitoring, the office of the Committee of Comprehensive Management of Social Order of Xin'anjiang Subdistrict of Jiande (Zhejiang) and the Xin'anjiang Police Station jointly carried out night patrol together with the in-service Party members and the retired Party members.

opinions. To make the decision more scientific, serious considerations should be given to the differing views of a minority and the reasonable ones shall be taken. In case of controversy over major issues in which supporters of the two opposing views are nearly equal in number, the decision should be put off to allow for further investigation and study followed by another vote.

That "the lower Party organizations are subordinate to the higher Party organizations" means lower Party organizations must firmly implement the decisions of higher Party organizations. If lower organizations consider that any decisions of higher organizations do not suit the specific conditions in their localities or departments, they may demand modifications. If the higher organizations insist on their original decisions, the lower organizations must carry out such decisions and refrain from publicly voicing their differences. However, there is a precondition that the leadership organs at all levels must solicit opinions from the lower Party organizations before making any important decision and shall not intervene in any affairs under the jurisdiction of the lower Party organizations. In addition, the lower Party organization has the right to report to the next higher Party organization.

That "all the constituent organizations and members of the Party are subordinate to the National Congress and the Central Committee of the Party" means the National Congress and the Central Committee elected by it are the highest leading body of the Party. Only the Central Committee of the Party has the power to make decisions on major policies of a nationwide character. Party organizations of various departments and localities may make suggestions with regard to such policies to the Central Committee, but shall not make any decisions or publicize their views outside the Party without authorization.

These provisions regulate behaviors of the Party members and Party organizations of all levels, allow for harmonious and consistent functions of the whole organizational system, and ensure thorough implementation of decisions made by the leading bodies at various levels while avoiding problems such as

On November 22, 2013, the representatives of the Party members at the Jinlong Community of Jinlong Township (Longmatan District, Luzhou, Sichuan) were taking a vote by show of hands.

deliberation without decision, making decisions without implementing them, willful actions, or even anarchy.

In summary, the system of democratic centralism combines advantages of democracy and efficiency. It can balance all interest demands of all parties concerned, facilitate proper combination of interests between the individual and the collective, the partial and the whole, the immediate and the long-term, and properly handle the relations between the leadership and the masses, democracy and legal system, discipline and freedom, and rights and obligations. Meanwhile, designing right principles and important decisions with the right centralism on the basis of democracy can form a unified willpower across the whole Party and the whole country, effectively integrate social resources, efficiently carry out the decisions, avoid various drawbacks and obstacles and help development and prosperity of China. It is with the scientific organizational principle can the CPC, which has more than 80 million members and millions of primary organizations, run flexibly and efficiently and play a core role in all the undertakings of modern China.

Primary Organizations

In addition to the scientific organizational principle, the strict organizational system is also an important factor ensuring the efficient operation of the CPC. From the development course of the CPC, it can be found that the founding of the CPC was under strong influence of the governing party of the only socialist county at that time – the Communist Party of Russia and the organizational structure of the CPC was also established with reference to the Russia's. After more than 90 years, the basic framework of the CPC's institutional framework does not change, although there are some important changes to the detailed organizational institutions. It still consists of three parts: the primary organizations, local organizations and central organizations.

The organizational system of the CPC has many characteristics. One of the distinctive points is that no Party member is allowed to stay out of the management of the organization. According to the *Constitution of the CPC*, every Party member must be organized into a branch and actively work in the branch. A branch is the smallest unit of the organizational system of the CPC. In the enterprises, villages, organs, schools, scientific research institutions, sub-district communities, social organizations, companies of the People's Liberation Army, and other primary organizations, a branch is set up when there are three or more full Party members. If an organization has only one or two Party members, they can set up a joint branch with a nearby organization. Normally the number of the members of a branch will not exceed 50. When the Party members of the branch exceed 50, it can apply to the higher Party committee for setting up a general branch with several branches. In the primary organizations, when the number of the Party members exceeds 100, committees of general Party branches or Party branches are set up subject to approval from the higher Party organizations. Party

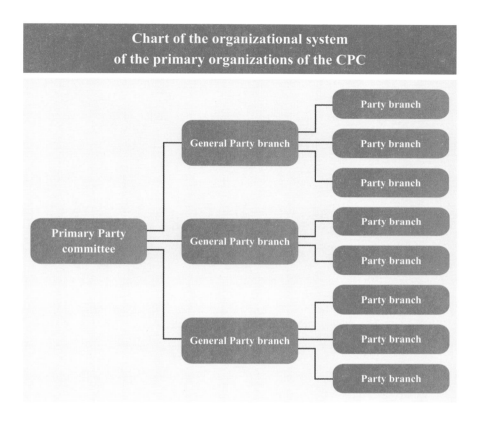

Chart of the organizational system of the primary organizations of the CPC

branch, general Party branch and primary Party committee actually form the primary organizational system of the CPC (see the figure above).

Although the Party branch is small in size, it plays a very important role in the whole organizational system of the CPC. First of all, a branch is an antenna of the CPC in the primary level of society and a connector connecting the political Party and the common people of all classes and in sectors. Second, lower in level in the organizational system, the branch undertakes many responsibilities such as disseminating the ideology, admitting Party members and mobilizing the masses as the end executor of all the lines, principles and policies of the CPC. Third, as the branch has a small number of the Party members, it is easy to manage, and can organize various programs timely and flexibly. Finally, the small size

The Party branch of Guhuai Street School (Xuchang, Henan) launches the Party's mass line learning activity through Wechat.

and high flexibility enable the branch to become an important "weapon" for the CPC to adapt to the high mobility and diversification trend of the society in the 21st century. At present, the CPC has broken the original pattern of setting up branches only in enterprises, schools and organs and other entities and started to set up such organizations in buildings, markets, industrial parks, communities and temporary settlements. The adjustment can not only prevent floating and dispersing Party members from staying away from the Party organizations, but also help the CPC constantly increase coverage of the primary organizations and fully mobilize the resources of the whole society in the context of increasing marketization of China.

The Party branches are the foundation of the whole organizational system of the CPC. However, with this organizational mode only, it cannot ensure unified action and active participation of all members of the Party branches in works. It needs a strong leadership. Just as the Chinese saying goes, "a train runs

On February 15, 2014, the first Party branch of the Voluntary Association of Jiangxi is established in Yushan County.

fast because of a good locomotive". Similarly, a political organization, regardless of its size, needs a core figure or leading body. According to regulations of the CPC, when the number of the Party members of a branch is less than 7, it does not need to set up a leading body. When the number reaches or exceeds 7, a Party committee shall be set up to lead works of the Party branch. The Party branch committee is not appointed by the higher Party organization, but elected by voting by all the Party members of the branch. In the same way, the committee of general Party branch which consists of many branches shall be elected by voting at the meeting by all Party members of the general Party branch. Now that the members of the committee are elected, there will be candidates. There are two ways to be candidates of the members of the Party branch committee: self-recommendation and recommendation by the higher Party organization. Normally the number of candidates shall be higher than the vacancies for competitive election. The Party branch committee or general Party branch committee is not a life-long term, but a term of two or three years. Therefore, if the Party branch committee does not fulfill its duties in the tenure, the Party members will elect a capable one in the election at the expiration of the office term to form a new Party branch committee. In this way, the Party branch committees can be headed to work actively and carefully to fulfill their duties.

The primary Party committees are the leading bodies of the CPC in the primary organizations. The methods of candidate recommendation and election procedure of the primary Party committees are similar to that of the Party branch committee and the general Party branch committee except for two points: first, the tenure of the primary Party committees is longer than the Party branch committee and the general Party branch committee. According to the *Opinions on the Tenure of the Primary Party Organizations of the Organization Department of the Central Committee of the CPC*, the Party committees of the large- and medium-sized enterprises, colleges and universities, large scientific research

On November 21, 2013, Party members of Shuimowan Village, Shajing Town, Ganzhou District, Zhangye, Gansu, elected the new Party branch committee with the "election based on two recommendations".

institutions, and the Party committees of the prefecture (city, league) level Party organs and those above the prefecture level are elected for a term of four years, while the other primary Party committees are elected for a term of three years. Second, as the number of Party members of the primary organizations is different, the primary Party committees can be elected by a general membership meeting or a meeting of delegates. That means when the number of the Party members is small, the primary Party committees can be elected directly by all Party members; and when the number is large, the Party branches and general Party branches can elect delegates to form a meeting of delegates and indirectly elect the primary Party committee. With increasing requirements on the democratic rights of the Party members at the primary organizations in recent years, the CPC made continuous exploration and designed two ways of election: "election based on two recommendations" and "public nomination and direct election".

The "election based on two recommendations" means the candidates of the Party branch committees are nominated by the democratic recommendation of the Party members and the masses and then elected with secret ballot by all Party members with the right to vote. The recommendation of Party members is the first step. The primary Party branch holds a general membership meeting and allows the Party members to recommend candidates for the new Party branch committee according to the positions and conditions of the new Party branch committee with secret recommendation (when the new Party branch committee has three members, the number of candidates recommended by every Party member shall not exceed three). The candidates will be decided according to the votes of the Party members (generally the number of candidates shall be higher than the number to be elected. It is subject to the actual situation). Then the mass delegates can recommend candidates at the villagers' or community meeting. The coverage can be expanded according to the actual situation of the villages or communities to the representatives of the Elderly's Associations and women's federation etc. In this way the primary Party branch can be recognized by the

Party members and the masses at the primary level of society to consolidate the foundation of ruling of the CPC as a governing party.

The "public nomination and direct election" is a new way of democratic election in the primary Party democracy building. "Public nomination" refers to that the Party members and the masses nominate members of the leading body of the primary Party organizations in public. It is an initial nomination with the purpose of increasing the legitimacy foundation of the leading body of the primary Party organizations. "Direct election" means election of secretary and deputy secretary of the primary Party organization in a direct way. It is an issue related to free choice of the Party members to reflect the willingness of the voters in a better way. Since 2001, Sichuan and some other provinces have elected the Party committee of the towns and townships with this method on a trial basis, receiving a good effect. In 2008 Chongqing especially promulgated the *Measures on Public Nomination and Direct Election of Members of Primary*

On December 20, 2013, the Party members of the Party branch of the Individual Labors' Association of Jintang Island of Zhoushan (Zhejiang) got together to elect the new Party branch committee through direct election.

Party Committees of Chongqing (Trial) which made detailed provisions on the candidate qualifications, recommendation methods and election procedure and promoted this in more than 80% of the towns and townships. On May 15, 2009, Shenzhen took a lead in applying "public nomination and direct election" in the election of secretary of the Party committees of the institutional organs and elected members, secretary, deputy secretary of the Party committee and secretary of the commission for discipline inspection of the institutional organs. The promotion of public nomination and direct election enables the Party members to exercise their democratic rights and stimulate their enthusiasm to care about the Party affairs; meanwhile it creates a fair, open and just competition environment for the talent to become eminent.

According to the CPC, if the organizational foundation of a political party is not well built, the whole party is weak. Therefore the CPC has attached great importance to the building and development of the primary Party organizations since its inception. As of the end of 2012, the Party organizations have been set up in 7,245 sub-district offices, 33,000 towns and townships, 87,000 communities (neighborhood committees), 588,000 villages, and 99.97% of the government organs, 99.4% of the institutions and 99.98% of the public-owned enterprises. What's more, the Party organizations have been set up in 1.475 million of non-public-owned enterprises, or 99.95% of the total conditional non-public-owned enterprises, 40,300 social organizations, or 99.21% of the total qualified social organizations, 39,500 private non-enterprise organizations, or 99.61% of the qualified private non-enterprise organizations. As of the end of 2010, the CPC has set up 3.892 million of primary Party organizations, including 187,000 primary Party committees, 242,000 general Party committees and 3.463 million Party branch committees. In addition to the large quantity, the CPC has also attached importance to the coverage of primary Party organizations in the grassroots society. By the end of 2010, the CPC has set up Party organizations in 6,869 sub-district offices, 34,000 towns and townships, 82,000 communities (neighborhood committees), and 594,000 villages. Among the villages and communities, the coverage of the primary Party organizations reached 99.9%. At the same time, 749,600 of the 750,700 enterprises, or 99.9% of the total, that have the conditions to set up primary Party organizations have set up the Party organizations. Of the 235,900 government organs that have the conditions to set up primary Party organizations, 235,800 organs, or 99.96% of the total, have set up Party organizations. And 492,600 of the 498,300 institutions, or 98.9%, have set up the Party organizations. The coverage of primary Party organizations in the colleges and universities reached 99.9%. While retaining the original foundation, the CPC has also made achievements in building primary Party organizations in the new social organizations and new economic organizations. In 2010, 14,200 of the 14,700 social organizations have set up primary Party organizations (96.8%). Of the 19,300 private non-enterprise organizations that have conditions to set up primary Party organizations, 18,900 organizations, or 98%, of them have set up. Obviously the CPC has set up a wide, strict and strong primary Party organization system.

In June 2008, the members of a "commando" consisted of the Party members of an airborne troop were taking the oath during the process of earthquake relief at Hanwang Town, Mianzhu, Sichuan.

Innovation has been made in setting up primary Party organizations with an expanded coverage. On the basis of establishing primary Party organizations by region and by unit, the CPC has constantly expanded the working coverage of the Party organizations by means of establishing Party organizations independently, jointly by different regions or different sectors or by means of dispatching the Party building mentor after establishing the mass organizations. The number of the Party organizations in the non-public-owned enterprises that have conditions to set up Party organizations increased 18.8% in 2012 against the previous year. And the coverage of Party organizations increased 1.8% and 0.3% in the social organizations and private non-enterprise organizations compared with the previous year.

The primary Party organizations are militant bastions of the Party and have given full play to the exemplary and vanguard role of the Party members. They organize, unite and head Party members and the masses to carry out the Party's line, principles and policies, fulfill various tasks, and give full play to its role in promoting development, serving the masses, uniting the people and enhancing harmony. Efforts have been made to promote Party members to emerge in their work in the window units and the service sector. In 2012, the Party organizations and Party members established 20.978 million of helping pairs with the masses and handled 49.628 million of affairs. In the important missions such as earthquake disaster relief, the Party members have played the exemplary and vanguard role and fully demonstrated the excellent quality and style of the times.

Local Organizations of the Party

Above the primary Party organizations which consist of the Party branches, general Party branches and the primary Party committees are the local organizations of the CPC. The local organization system of the Party is established mainly to correspond to the administrative division of China in three tiers: provinces, autonomous regions and municipalities are the first tier; cities with districts and autonomous prefectures are at the second tier, and the counties (banners), autonomous counties, cities without districts and urban districts are at the third tier. There are Party delegate meetings and Party committees of the same level at each tier. They are the leading bodies of the CPC at the level with a term of five years. A general election will be held every five years.

The Party congresses at their respective levels consist of the Party member delegates and execute rights on behalf of the Party members, mainly including: to hear and examine the reports of the Party committees at the corresponding levels; to hear and examine the reports of the commissions for discipline inspection at the corresponding levels; to discuss and adopt resolutions on major issues in the given areas; and to elect the Party committees and commissions for discipline inspection at the corresponding levels.

To ensure the representativeness of the Party delegates, the CPC has made provisions on the following three aspects: first, only the advanced model Party members can be elected as the Party delegates. How to evaluate the excellence of the Party members? The Party member delegate can carry out the Party's lines, principles and policies; handle affairs following the Party's principles; guard Party secrets and have certain capability of offering useful opinions. Second, the Party member delegates of the Party congresses at various levels must represent the interests of the majority of the people, not just the interests of a part of the

Delegates heard and examined the report made by Secretary of the CPC Beijing Municipal Committee at the 11th Congress of the CPC of Beijing on June 29, 2012.

Party members. Therefore, the Party congresses of various levels must have delegates of leaders and cadres, professionals and technicians, and advanced models of various sectors, PLA and armed forces. The proportion of delegates of women and ethnic minority shall be no lower than the proportion of the women and ethnic minority Party members in the total Party members. Third, the delegates of the Party congresses shall be elected with the bottom-to-top method on the precondition of full intra-Party democracy. In line with the election regulations of local organizations of the Party, the Party congresses of provinces, autonomous regions and municipalities normally have 400 to 800 Party member delegates; the Party congresses of cities with districts and autonomous prefecture normally have 300 to 500 delegates; the Party congresses of counties (banners), autonomous counties, urban districts and districts normally have 200 to 400 delegates. Before starting the election procedure, local Party committees will allocate the quota to the election units according to number of the Party members and Party organizations. Then the election units decide the candidates of delegates according to opinions of the majority of the Party organizations and Party members.

For example, the delegate candidates of the counties (banners), autonomous counties, cities without districts and urban districts are decided in the following way: first, the primary Party branches convene a meeting to decide the delegate candidates according to opinions of the majority of the Party members and report the result to the primary Party committees. The primary Party committees select candidates from all the recommended candidates according to opinions of the majority of the Party branches and publicize the list of the selected candidates to solicit opinions from the Party branches and Party members, and then report the list of the recommended candidates to the Party committees of the counties (cities, or districts) according to the solicited opinions. The Party committees of the counties (cities, or districts) select candidates from the recommended list and publicize the list to solicit opinions from the primary Party committees which submit their opinions after full discussion to the Party committees of the counties (cities, or districts). The Party committees of the counties (cities, or districts) decide the list of candidates with at least 20% of surplus for competitive election according to the solicited opinions, and then publicize the list to the primary Party committees. The delegate candidates of the Party congresses of the provinces, autonomous regions, municipalities, cities with districts and autonomous prefectures are selected in the same way.

After the delegate candidates are decided, the primary Party committees make full observation to the delegates one by one and report the results to the higher Party committees. Then the election units convene the general membership meeting or Party congress, or conference of delegates to elect delegates from those candidates who are confirmed qualified to take part in the higher Party congress. This bottom-to-top step-by-step Party member delegate selection method gives full play to the spirit of democracy and ensures expression of opinions of the Party members and masses in the Party congress.

The local Party committees at all levels shall, when the Party congresses of the given areas are not in session, carry out the resolutions of the Party congresses at the corresponding levels and directives of the next higher Party organizations, implement the Party's lines, principles and policies and laws and regulations of the central government, direct work in their own areas on the political, economic, cultural and social development and report on it to the higher Party committees at regular intervals. The local Party committees consist of full members and alternate members and the number of alternate members is no less than 15% of the total number of full members. The alternate members have the priority to become full member of the Party committees of the same level. That means if any full member of the Party committees of the same level passes away, resigns or is dismissed, the alternate member can become the full member. The local Party committees are the leading bodies of the given area and shall be responsible for the economic and social development of the area, making decisions on important issues with regard to the Party's self-building and other missions, and recommending cadres to the local government organs, setting up Party organizations in the local government organs, people's organizations, economic and cultural organizations and other non-CPC organizations, and mobilizing and organizing Party organizations and Party members to fulfill missions allocated by the higher Party organizations.

However, the local Party committees at all levels meet in plenary session at least twice a year but are not a standing institution. The local Party committees at all levels elect, at their plenary sessions, their standing committees, secretaries and deputy secretaries. The standing committees of the local Party committees at all levels exercise the functions and powers of local Party committees when the latter are not in session. They continue to handle the day-to-day work when the next Party congresses at their levels are in session, until the new standing

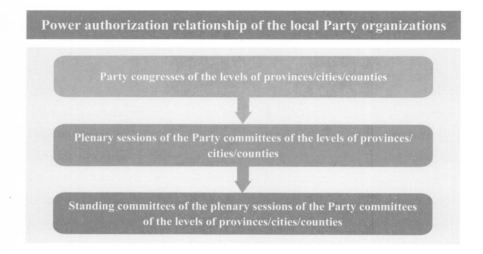

committees are elected. From the authorization relationship between the Party congresses and the Party committees and their standing committees at the respective levels (see the figure below), we can found that it is the standing committee that administrates the day-to-day work and exercises important functions in the local works.

The standing committee meetings are convened and presided over by the secretary of the Party committees twice a month or any time in case of important issues. If the secretary cannot take part in the meeting, the deputy secretary can be entrusted to convene and preside over the meeting. It has the right to make decisions on not only important issues in the day-to-day work about the economic and social development and the Party building, but also issues asked by the Party organizations of the government organs of the same level, people's organizations, economic organizations, cultural organizations and the leading bodies of non-Party organizations. Meanwhile, it can ask for instructions and report to the higher Party organizations in the name of the Party committee, issue instructions, notices and circulars and other important documents to the subordinate Party organizations in the name of the Party committees, recommend, nominate, appoint, dismiss, educate and supervise cadres in line with the cadre management jurisdiction and designated procedure and transfer or assign the responsible person of the next subordinate Party organizations.

However, the rights of the standing committees are under certain restrictions. The *Constitution of the CPC* stipulates that the standing committees of the local Party committees at all levels regularly report their work to plenary sessions of local Party committees and accept their supervision. This provision has attracted increasing attentions from the local Party organizations. In 2005, the CPC Sichuan Provincial Committee especially designed the *Interim Provisions of Sichuan Province on Reporting Work to and Accepting Supervision from the Plenary Sessions for Standing Committees of Cities (Prefectures) and Counties (Cities, Districts)* (hereinafter referred to as Interim Provisions), requiring the standing committees to submit the working report to the plenary sessions five days in advance for delegates to have sufficient time to read through and study the report. If the working report is not adopted, the standing committees shall prepare a new report within three months and notify the subordinate Party organizations about the working report in a proper way. To facilitate supervision of the members of the Party committees to the standing committees, the Interim Provisions emphasize that the members can question or inquire for explanation about the working report and they will not be investigated for any speech made at the deliberation of the working report of the standing committees. In 2012, the CPC Guangdong Provincial Committee distributed the *Interim Provisions on Giving Full Play to the Plenary Sessions of Party Committees at Various Levels of Guangdong Province*, and pointed out that when the plenary session is not in session, delegates of the plenary session shall actively take part in the special supervision, check unhealthy tendencies and malpractices, and make secret investigation to check nonfeasance and other problems. As to resolutions of the plenary sessions or issues arising from implementation of the resolutions, the delegates of the plenary session of the Party committees can question or inquire in writing the standing committees of the Party committees of the same level, the discipline inspection commissions, functional departments, affiliated organizations, dispatched organs, dispatched tour inspection bodies, Party committees (leadership groups) established with approval from the local Party committees in line with the relevant previsions, stipulated in the Opinions. Those who are questioned or inquired shall make explanation in writing to the plenary session within the designated time. In addition, delegates of the plenary session can attend the meetings of the standing committees of the Party committees of the same level as a non-voting delegate and express opinions and offer suggestions on the topics of the meetings.

While giving full play to the functions of the plenary sessions of the Party committees, the Party has carried out the permanent tenure system in some cities, counties and districts on a trial basis since the late 1980s to further enlarge the intra-Party democracy and guard the rights of the Party congress. In this process, many methods and ways have been developed to improve the intra-Party

On November 5, 2012, the Party members at the Tianyihe Care Home (Nankai District, Tianjin) made 1,300 silk flowers symbolizing 1.3 billion people and 56 rose flowers symbolizing 56 ethnic groups, showing their loyalty to the Party and their determination to contribute to the construction of a bright future.

democracy quality in various regions. For example, Baixia District, Nanjing, Jiangsu Province, has allowed delegates to have more direct communications and connections with the Party members of the given electoral area in the process of promoting the permanent tenure system. Consequently the Party members have increased recognition to the delegates. Jiaojiang District, Taizhou, Zhejiang Province set up the permanent tenure system of the district to receive delegates of the primary Party congress, allow the delegate to attend meetings of the Party committees as non-voting delegates and offer suggestions and opinions, and other system to enforce rights of the delegates, stimulated initiatives, enthusiasm and creativity of the Party members to promote economic and social development. As a result, Jiaojiang District ranked the first in Taizhou in the social and economic development in 2007. Dunhuang of Gansu Province organized delegates of the city and township levels to carry out ten initiatives such as "100-day investigation of national conditions", investigation and visit, and evaluate advanced model Party members from 2008 to 2012, handled more than 320 pieces of opinions and suggestions of the Party members and the masses, implemented 26 aiding programs with a financial input of more than 3.6 million yuan, and conducted more than 450 matters directly related to the livelihood of the people. On this basis, the 18th National Congress of the CPC emphasized that efforts should be made to deepen the permanent tenure system of the Party congress on a trial basis and implement the motion system. Within a year, the program has rolled out across China, significantly improved the cohesion and creativity of the local Party organizations.

Central Organizations of the Party

The central organizations of the Party stand on the top of the CPC organizational system and are responsible for the leadership of all works of the Party. The highest leading body of the Party is the National Congress, which is convened once every five years, and its Central Committee. The Central Commission for Discipline Inspection elected by the National Congress is the highest discipline inspection body of the Party. The National Congress, the Central Committee and the Central Commission for Discipline Inspection are of great significance to the Party and China as a whole. Therefore the Party has attached great importance to delegates or members. This is explained by taking the 18th National Congress of the CPC convened in November 2012 as an example.

Delegates took group photo in front of the Great Hall of the People as the 18th National Congress of the CPC was concluded in Beijing on November 14, 2012.

According to the *Constitution of the CPC*, the number of delegates of the National Congress of the CPC and the election method are subject to the Central Committee of the CPC. In November 2011, a year before the 18th National Congress of the CPC was convened, the Central Committee issued the *Circular on Election of the Delegates of the 18th National Congress of the CPC* to deploy election works of the National Congress. Taking the increase of the primary Party organizations and Party members in the five years after the 17th National Congress and the necessity of increasing number of delegates at the front line of production and works into considerations, the number of delegates of the 18th National Congress was decided to be 2,270, an increase of 50 delegates compared with that of the 17th National Congress of the CPC.

According to the Circular, 31 provinces (autonomous regions and municipalities), organs directly under the Central Committee of the CPC, the central state organs, All- China Federation of Taiwan Compatriots, People's Liberation Army, the Armed Police Force, the financial system of central government, central enterprises, the Hong Kong working committee of the CPC, Macao working committee of the CPC, 40 election units in total, started to elect delegates tier by tier. In order to truly reflect the will of all Party members, the election units widely disseminated the great significance and policies of delegate election of the 18th National Congress of the CPC by means of distributing outlines, sending SMS, posting public letters to the Party members and other instruments to organize and mobilize the Party members, including floating Party members, and retired Party members to participate in the nomination of delegates. Statistics indicated that nearly all the Party organizations of the election units were involved, and 98% of the Party members attended the work.

In order to ensure that the delegates are elected in a standard and serious way, the Central Committee of the CPC defined the election procedure that mainly includes five steps: candidate recommendation and nomination, observation to candidates, deciding the primary list of candidates and publicizing the list, deciding the tentative list of candidates, convening a general membership meeting or a meeting of delegates to elect delegates. In line with the requirements of the five steps, the Organization Department of the Central Committee of the CPC detailed procedures of each step and worked out a flow chart of the delegate election of the 18th National Congress of the CPC for the election units to follow.

With more than a half year, 2,270 delegates were elected and finalized in July 2012. These delegates were elected from various areas and sectors, covering economy, science and technology, national defense, politics and law, education, publicity, culture, healthcare, sports and social management and other fields, consisting of leaders, cadres, Party members at the front line of production and work, workers, farmers, technicians, servicemen, cadres of primary organizations and management personnel of enterprises and institutional organizations and the Party members from the non-public-owned enterprises and new social organizations. Of that, 1,578 were leaders and cadres (69.5%), 692 were Party

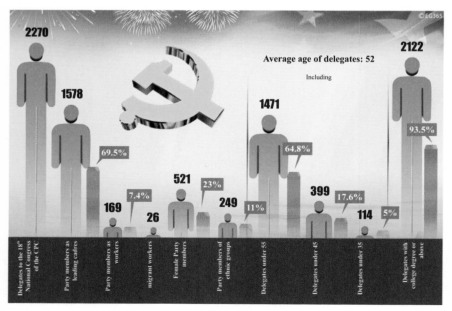

Structure of the delegates of the 18th National Congress of the CPC.

members from the front line of production and work (30.5%); and 1,471 Party members were below 55 year old (64.8%), 399 Party members below 45 years old (17.6%), and 114 below 35 years old (5%).

During the session of the National Congress, the delegates have the right to hear and examine the reports of the Central Committee; to hear and examine the reports of the Central Commission for Discipline Inspection; to discuss and decide on major questions concerning the Party; to revise the Constitution of the Party; to elect the Central Committee; and to elect the Central Commission for Discipline Inspection. When the National Congress is not in session, the Central Committee carries out its resolutions, directs the entire work of the Party and represents the Communist Party of China in its external relations. The Party's Central Commission for Discipline Inspection functions under the leadership of the Central Committee of the Party and is responsible for the following tasks: to uphold the Constitution and other statutes of the Party, to assist Party committees in improving Party's style of work and to check up on the implementation of the line, principles, policies and resolutions of the Party, to provide education for the Party members on their duty to observe Party discipline and adopt decisions for the upholding of Party discipline, to examine and deal with relatively important or complicated cases of violation of the Constitution or other statutes of the Party by Party organizations or Party members and decide on or rescind disciplinary measures against Party members involved in such cases, and deal with complaints and appeals made by Party members.

The election of the Central Committee and the Central Commission for Discipline Inspection was an important mission of the National Congress of the CPC. For example, for the 18th National Congress of the CPC, Hu Jintao, then general secretary of the Central Committee of the CPC presided over the meeting of the Central Political Bureau Standing Committee and the meeting of the Central Political Bureau to decide the guiding thinking and principles for election of the Central Committee and the Central Commission for Discipline Inspection,

On November 8, 2012, teachers and students of Hubei University of Economics watched the live broadcast of the 18th National Congress of the CPC at the classrooms, conference rooms and electronic reading rooms.

define the general requirements and qualification of candidates, structure of and recommendation and observation methods. Finally the 17th Central Committee of the CPC made the following resolutions:

——The new Central Committee shall be a group of politicians who are armed with the Marxism-Leninism, Mao Zedong Thought, Deng Xiaoping Theory and the important thought of Three Represents, who must thoroughly implement the scientific outlook on development, firmly implement the Party's basic line, basic principles and basic experience, and unswervingly take the road of socialism with Chinese characteristics. What's more, it must serve the people wholeheartedly, steadfastly build itself for public interests, exercise governance for the people, and seek truth from facts, stick to reform and innovation, and thrifty and perseverance. It shall remain honest and upright, and is highly unified ideologically, politically and organizationally, so that it will stand forever in the forefront of the times and can handle comprehensive situations, cope with various challenges and head all the peoples to constantly promote the socialist economic development, political development, cultural development, social development and ecological civilization development and the Party building.

——The new Central Commission for Discipline Inspection shall be a leading body which will decisively carry through the Party's line, principles and policies, and is good at mastering the overall situation of anti-corruption and stepping up efforts to improve its style of work and uphold integrity. With firm ideal and belief, strong Party spirit. iIt shall be fair and honest, and has the courage to uphold the principles and fight against a variety of violations of laws and disciplines and malpractices.

In line with the unified deployment of the Central Committee, from July 2011 to June 2012, the Central Committee dispatched 59 observation teams to 31 provinces (autonomous regions and municipalities) and 130 organs directly under the Central Committee and the central government, central financial institutions and central enterprises in Beijing. The Central Military Commission dispatched nine observation teams to the PLA and the Armed Police Force. Latter, additional observation was made to some candidates. Statistics indicate that the observation teams made democratic recommendations among more than 428,000 candidates, and talked with more than 27,500 candidates. The main leaders of the provincial (autonomous region, municipality) committees of the CPC proposed the tentative list of the observation objects according to the democratic recommendations and candidate structure at the proportion of 1:1.5-2. The team leaders and the main leaders of the provincial (autonomous region, municipality) committees of the CPC exchanged views purposely with the candidates according to the actual situation. Opinions were solicited from individuals or at the meetings of the standing committees. Then the list of observation objects was decided according to opinions solicited and votes of the Party congress or enlarged session. For the Central Committee, state organs and other parties concerned, the observation teams proposed the tentative list of observation for competitive or non-competitive observation according to the democratic recommendations to further solicit opinions from members of Party leadership group (Party committee) or meetings of the Party leadership group (Party committee) of the observation units. Some observation units held the Party leadership group (Party committee) meetings to vote for the candidates of the tentative list according to the actual situation. The list of observation objects was decided according to the opinions solicited and votes of the Party leadership group (Party committee).

From the second half of 2011 to the second half of 2012, the Central Political Bureau Standing Committee of the CPC convened 11 meetings to hear reports of the observation teams to master information of the observation results. In October 2012, the Central Political Bureau Standing Committee of the CPC finally decided the tentative list of 532 candidates from 727 candidates finalized by the observation teams with comprehensive consideration and research and then submitted the list to the National Congress for formal election. The plenary sessions of the Central Committee shall be convened at least once a year. However, when the Central Committee is not in session, the Political Bureau elected by it in plenary session and its Standing Committee will exercise the functions and powers of the Central Committee. In contrast, the local Party organizations will elect a standing committee of the Party congress, which is the difference between the central Party organizations and the local Party organizations. There are some other differences in the organizational structure (see the Figure below).

When the Central Committee is not in session, the central Party organizations including the top leaders and the Political Bureau, Standing Committee of the Political Bureau and the Central Military Commission are all elected in the plenary sessions of the Central Committee. Of that, general secretary of the Central Committee of the CPC is the official title of the top leader of the CPC, responsible for convening the meetings of the Political Bureau

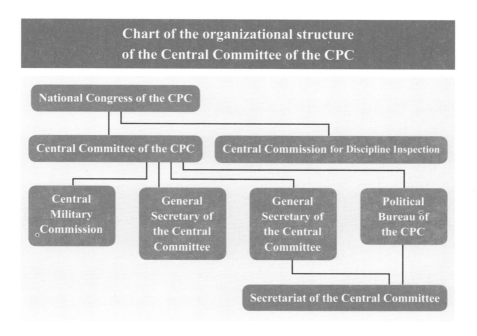

Chart of the organizational structure
of the Central Committee of the CPC

and its Standing Committee and is in charge of the work of the Secretariat. When the Central Committee is not in session, the Political Bureau and its Standing Committee exercise the functions and powers of the Central Committee. Considering the heavy works, the Secretariat of the Central Committee is established as the working body of the Political Bureau of the Central Committee and its Standing Committee. The members of the Secretariat are nominated by the Standing Committee of the Political Bureau of the Central Committee and are subject to endorsement by the Central Committee in plenary session. The Central Military Commission is the highest military leading body under the leadership of the Central Committee of the CPC and directly heads the armed force of the whole country. Considering its special position in the leadership structure of the CPC, the members of the Military Commission of the Central Committee are decided by the Central Committee, not by election.

Leadership Style and Governance

Any ruling party cannot achieve the purpose of governance or fulfill the historic mission of leading a country's development relying only on its own efforts. Instead, it must attach great importance to controlling and employing the organization of the state power and pooling the strength and wisdom of external parties and social groups. The CPC is no exception and has something different from other parties: It is not only a ruling party, but also a leading party. Therefore, how to address the relations between the two roles, better lead the country's development and realize the ruling objectives become the issues that the CPC has to face. During the exploration, the CPC has kept improving its style of leadership and style of governance, in a bid to increase governance efficiency and establish its image as a sound ruling party.

Assume a Dominant Role,
Co-ordinate Different Parties

During the period from the founding of the New China to the third plenary session of the 11th Central Committee of the CPC, the centralized leadership featuring no separation between the Party work and the government work and substituting the government with the Party were the main way of operation of the CPC. As the new period began, the second generation of the central collective leadership with Comrade Deng Xiaoping at the core realized the disadvantages of the leadership system to the country's development. Hence, it decided to make it one of the core contents of China's political reform to improve the Party's leadership and separate the Party work from government work, constantly enhanced the Party's leadership system and work mechanism, and gradually accelerated the restoration and optimization of the system of multiparty cooperation and political consultation under the leadership of the CPC, which greatly promoted improvements in both the socialist system and the style of governance of the CPC. In the 21st century, the CPC, while cementing its leading position, consistently regulated its relations with the people's congress, government and CPPCC in the principle of exercising overall leadership and coordinating the efforts of all.

First, the organizational structure and work mechanism featuring "one ore and three Party groups" have been established and improved. "One core" means the Party committee shall play its core leading role in organizations at various levels. This actually covers two sides: First, any major issues that have comprehensive, strategic, fundamental or forward-looking implications in local regions or authorities shall be discussed by the Party committee to ensure no divergence from the right path; second, the Party committee cannot replace other organizations in actual work, with the leading role mainly reflected in political, ideological and organizational leadership. That is, it shall develop major guidelines, give legislation suggestions, recommend key cadres and carry out ideological publicity to give play to the role of both Party organizations and Party members, rather than lead everything either important or trivial. "Three Party groups" refers to putting in place Party groups respectively in the people's congress, government and CPPCC as the organizational form to realize the core leading role and governance purpose of the Party committee. As stipulated in the Party Constitution, Party groups can be set up in the leadership of both central and local authorities, people's organizations, economic organizations, cultural organizations and other non-Party organizations. Such Party groups are responsible for implementing the Party's lines, guidelines and policies, discussing and deciding major issues of respective organizations, doing a good job in cadre management, uniting the cadres and mass outside the Party, fulfilling the tasks assigned by the Party and State, and guiding work of Party groups in

The Second Session of the 12th National People's Congress opened on March 13, 2014 at the Great Hall of the People. The picture shows the deputies are applauding for the wonderful report.

directly affiliated organizations. Members of Party groups are appointed and led by as well as responsible for the Party committees that approve setup of the Party groups. However, Party groups are not first-level organizations of the Party, but dispatched agencies of Party organizations and thus have no independent right to develop Party members.

Under the work mechanism, the CPC doesn't issue orders directly to the people's congress, government and CPPCC, but play its leading role through the Party groups set up in the organizations. Party group of the standing committee of the people's congress, on one hand, often reports to Party committee to learn about its intents in various work and thus turn the Party's decisions to State wills in a timely manner, and on the other hand, submits the decisions and resolutions to be passed by the standing committees of the people's congress as well as the key points of annual work and legislation plans of the standing committee in the draft form to Party committee for review and approval, so as to ensure no divergence of the work by the organ of State power from the correct political directions. In particular, the meetings of the people's congress, meeting agendas of the standing committee, legislation plans of the people's congress and the standing committee, political laws and major economic laws to be developed, major problems encountered during the process of law drafting, major divergences arising from legal review as well as major issues related to supervision and decision and cadre appointment and removal shall be submitted by the Party groups of the standing committee of the people's congress to the Party organization at a higher level for decision or enter legal procedures after approval. Given the fact that governments at various levels are the administrative enforcement agencies generated through elections at the people's congress, the Party group in government, first of all, shall support government in implementing resolutions of the people's congress, which are fundamentally consistent with the Party's guidelines and policies. The Party group of the CPPCC shall pay attention to all the democratic parties in the CPPCC and report important views of the democratic parties to Party committees in a timely manner in addition to reporting to Party committee the decisions to be passed and proposals to be submitted by the CPPCC. Meanwhile, it has the responsibility for actively communicating with other members of the CPPCC based on fully understanding the intents of Party committee, in a bid to make the Party's intents recognized by various sides.

Second, efforts have been made to recommend major cadres to the organs of State power for improvements of the Party's influence. Sending elites of a party to organs of political power and thus reflecting intents of the party during submission of proposals, formulation of laws as well as government decision-making and implementation serves as an approach for many ruling parties to control public power. In China, recommending members of the standing committees of the people's congress at the same level, members of the people's government, chief judges of the people's court, chief procurators of the people's procuratorate and other leaders and cadres appointed by local organs as managed by Party committee is a major responsibility of the CPC organizations at both central and local levels as well as one of the ways for the CPC to give play to its core leading role.

Surely, recommendation is made strictly in accordance with specified procedures. First, the organizations responsible for recommendation will hear opinions from various sides, including those from democratic parties, mass groups and nonparty personages, through democratic recommendation or democratic assessment to identify candidates to be investigated and organize investigation. Afterwards, the standing committee or all the members of Party committee will discuss and decide on the persons to be recommended and submit the results to the Party committee at a higher level for review and approval. After approval, Party committee will introduce the personnel arrangement as approved by the Party committee at a higher level to the Party groups in the organs of political power at the same level and Party members in the leadership of the organs of political power, and further hear opinions; It will inform

The Second Plenary Session of the First Meeting of the 12th CPPCC was held at the Great Hall of the People on March 7, 2013. The picture shows the rostrum.

heads of democratic parties and representatives of nonparty personages of relevant information for democratic consultation. It will also submit letters of recommendation to the presidium of the people's congress, explaining reasons for recommendation, introducing basic information about recommended persons and answering relevant questions. After final confirmation of recommended persons, organs of State power will make selection and appointment according to relevant procedures.

It's noteworthy that the Party committee has only the right to recommend rather than the right to make decisions or the right to appoint and dismiss. To increase the chance of having the recommended persons approved, the CPC developed rigid standards when first identifying candidates, so as to pick out the persons who are honest, public-spirited, qualified for the proposed jobs and trusted by the masses. After the recommended persons become leadership members of the NPC, government and CPPCC, they will earnestly execute various guidelines and policies of the Party in concrete work, thus realizing the leading role of the CPC as a ruling party. In fact, the behaviors of the leaders and cadres are reflection of the leading role of the CPC.

Third, efforts have been made to give play to the role of Party member and Party organizations in organs of State power in executing the Party's guidelines, lines and policies. The CPC has more than 80 million members, with those in organs of State power making up a big part. According to the Party Constitution, Party members must implement the Party's fundamental lines and various guidelines and policies, execute the Party's decisions and vigorously fulfill tasks assigned by the Party. Meanwhile, the Party Constitution provides that a grassroots Party organization shall be set up so long as the Party members number more than three. Therefore, there are a big number of grassroots Party organizations in various organs of State power. These grassroots Party organizations and Party members serve as key intermediaries for the CPC to play its core leading role. For example, after a Party committee recommends a candidate for a certain cadre post, the Party organization in the organ will organize its members to do a good job in introducing and publicizing the recommended person, and during voting, Party members will also make the same choice as the Party to realize the Party's intent. Such an approach also exists in some western political parties. Take the UK for example, as the central party organization outside the government has the right to dismiss parliamentarians from the party and prevent the party organization in the electoral ward from identifying him as the parliamentarian candidate of the party, parliamentarians will obey the requirements and proposals of the Party organizations outside the parliament unless they have to do so. Besides, in daily work and life, the CPC members will explain the Party's basic theories, lines, guidelines and policies to nonparty mass to improve their recognition of the Party; Meanwhile, they will tell Party organizations about the views and opinions of nonparty mass to make the Party learn about updates of workers in the organs and offer appropriate guidance. All these help the CPC give play to its core leading role.

While the CPC upholds the principle of the Party administrating cadres, China's Constitution provides that the people's congress and its standing committee have the right to elect, appoint and dismiss members of organs of State power and other public officials. Therefore, adhering to and improving the mechanism in which Party organizations recommend major cadres also involves effective support and guarantee for exercise of the right to appoint and dismiss by the people's congress and its standing committee. On such a basis, Party committee in the organs of State power must respect the election results of the people's congress and their standing committee. Even if the intents of recommendation aren't fully realized, Party organizations at various levels must observe the election results so long as the procedures are lawful.

Fourth, organs of State power have been supported in fulfilling their responsibilities. The CPC leadership is not one-way or coercive, but takes shape based on sound interactions. On one hand, the CPC keeps improving the way to play its leading role; On the other hand, the CPC has always supported all the

The 32nd Session of the Standing Committee of the 11th People's Congress of Shandong Province closed in Jinan on the afternoon of August 1, 2012, approving by voting relevant decisions as well as appointment and removal of officials.

On May 6, 2014, the local government of Tonglu County of Zhejiang held the Government Open Day activity. A total of 200 representatives of citizens visited the office of the local government and attended the meeting for the communication between the government and the people. The picture shows the leaders of the county are listening to the opinions and advice of the people.

organs of power in fulfilling their responsibilities in accordance with relevant laws and regulations and provided them with guarantee in various aspects to lay a sound foundation for the Party's leadership.

As for the people's congress, the CPC has always supported it in exercising their legislation function and improving legislation quality. Meanwhile, it consciously receives supervision from the people's congress, and pushes the people's congress to keep improving supervision mechanisms and systems and intensify effectiveness of supervision. It keeps deputies to the people's congress informed of developments in state affairs, and expand their participation in the activities of standing committees, in an effort to help deputies to the people's congress review proposals and reports, secure their right to know and improve their abilities and efficiency in reviewing proposals and reports.

As for the people's governments at various levels, the Central Committee of the CPC has made separation between Party work and government work as the core of the political system reform launched since China's reform and opening-up. More than re-defining the functions of the Party and government, it has also initiated several institutional reforms in government and urged government to lower administrative cost and improve work efficiency. Since the 16th National Congress of the CPC, it has pressed government to deepen the reform to the administrative system and helped it complete the transfer of role from an administrator to a service provider.

As for the CPPCC, Party committee at various levels actively communicate with the CPPCC at the same level to hear their opinions and suggestions when deciding major guidelines at the State and local levels as well as major issues in

On May 8, 2014, the officials of the procuratorate are listening to the opinions of the villagers of the Xiaoliangzhuang Village (Zhuji Town, Sheqi County, Henan) at the courtyard of Liang Xiaodong, a young person who started his own business at his hometown after graduation from school.

political, economic, cultural and social life. The CPC has always encouraged the plenary meetings, standing committee meetings and chairman meetings of the CPPCC to present suggestion proposals to Party committee and government, and encouraged special committee to give suggestions or reports on major issues; It supports CPPCC members in visiting grassroots organizations to learn about updates and report social conditions and public opinions. It earnestly addresses the proposals and suggestions submitted by CPPCC and gives official replies in a timely manner.

It is these systems and moves that support organs of the State power in fulfilling respective responsibilities according to law that ensure the sound operation of the State. While consolidating the core leading position of the CPC and ensuring implementation of the Party's resolutions and spirits in actual work, the systems and moves offer extensive support and power source for advance of the great cause of socialism with Chinese characteristics.

Governance for and by the People

As the old saying goes, "While water can keep a boat afloat, it can also overturn it." The CPC considers the people as water and itself as a boat with all the power sourced from the support and push of the people. Therefore, the CPC has developed clear understanding since the founding of the New China in 1949: It won the victory in Chinese revolution in the past by relying on the people, and could only achieve success in future governance equally by relying on the people; To gain public support, it must make safeguarding the fundamental interests of the people and earnestly improving their living standards as the essential goal of governance.

On April 3, 2014, Zhang Chunxian, member of the Political Bureau of the Central Committee of the CPC and Secretary of the CPC Committee of the Xinjiang Uygur Autonomous Region, visited Hutubi County. The picture shows Zhang is talking with the representatives of villagers at the Dongtan Village of the Ershilidian Town.

Since China's reform and opening-up, the CPC has been increasingly aware of governance and become ever firmer in the philosophy of governance for the people and relying on the people while constantly improving the style of leadership. In 1980 when China's reform and opening-up was just launched, Deng Xiaoping warned the whole Party that "all the Party organizations, members and cadres must merge with the masses and not stand on their opposite side. If a Party organization severely divorces from the masses and cannot correct it in a resolute manner, it is doomed to failure as it will lose the source of power and be abandoned by the people." In the 1990s when China's reform enters a fresh stage, Jiang Zemin once again reminded the whole Party that "our reform and construction can only advance smoothly by gaining the understanding, support and participation of the masses and giving full play to the enthusiasm and creativity of the masses; The Party's leadership can only be consolidated with the trust and support from the masses. Our Party will accomplish nothing and even cannot exist without support of the people." In 2004, Hu Jintao required the whole Party to "do everything for the masses and relying on the masses, to exercise the power for the people, empathize with the feelings of the people and work for the well-being of the people, and to make realizing, safeguarding and developing the fundamental interests of the overwhelming majority of the people as the very aim and fundamental end of all the work as well as the guarantee for doing every job well," and stressed that's what the whole Party must unswervingly adhered to at any time.

Only ideas that are combined with practices can play their role. In 2012, to increase the Party's awareness of governance for the people, the 18th National Congress of the CPC explicitly proposed to launch the campaign aimed to educate all the Party members about the Party's mass line with the pragmatic and clean governance for the people as the core. The campaign was initiated in the latter half of 2013 and expected to last for one year, with the leadership and cadres above the county level as the focus and the eight-point code to maintain

On April 17, 2013, young civil servants from the Huaying Office of the State Administration of Taxation were helping the farmers to transport rice seedlings.

close ties with the people and raise the Party's profile as proposed by Xi Jinping at the end of 2012 as the starting point:

First, efforts shall be made to improve investigations and researches and to learn about actual facts at grass-roots levels, summarizing experience, studying problems, solving difficulties and guiding advance of work. Efforts shall be made to learn from the masses and practices, to talk with the masses and cadres, to have more discussions and analyze typical cases, and to frequently visit the places where difficulties, contradictions and public opinions are concentrated, rather than go through the motions and pursue formalism. Efforts shall be made to reduce size of people in company during a visit and simplify reception, and to forbid hanging slogan and banners, organizing masses for welcoming and seeing-off ceremonies, laying welcoming carpets, placing decorative flowers and plants and arranging banquets.

Second, efforts shall be made to simplify meetings and improve meeting styles. National meetings and major activities held in the name of the Central Committee of the CPC must be strictly controlled; No meetings for abstract deployment and requirements shall be held, and no presence at any ribbon-cutting ceremonies, foundation-laying ceremonies, celebrations, commemorations, commendation meetings, expos, seminars and forums is allowed without approval from the Central Committee of the CPC; Efficiency of meetings shall be improved to make talks short and pragmatic rather than empty and stereo-typed.

Third, documents and bulletins shall be simplified and style of writing shall be improved. Documents and bulletins that have no substantial contents and can be either released or not released shall not be released.

Fourth, visiting activities shall be regulated. Foreign visits shall be arranged in a reasonable manner for diplomatic purposes; Numbers of accompanying staff shall be strictly controlled, and means of transport shall be in line with relevant regulations. Chinese-funded institutions, overseas Chinese and students studying abroad will not be arranged at airports for welcoming or seeing-off services in general.

Fifth, work of security guards shall be improved. Traffic control shall be reduced for the sake of achieving closer ties with the masses; No roads will be closed and no venues will be cleared in general.

Sixth, news coverage shall be improved. Whether presence of comrades of the Political Bureau of the CPC Central Committee at meetings or activities shall be covered depends on the needs of work, news values and social effects, and the quantities, number of words and time lengths of coverage shall be further reduced.

Seventh, release of articles shall be controlled. Unless arranged by the CPC Central Committee, individuals shall neither have works or speech monographs published, nor send letters or telegrams of congratulation or write inscriptions.

Eighth, thrift and economy shall be practiced, and regulations regarding clean governance shall be strictly followed, so shall be the regulations concerning housing and vehicle arrangement and other aspects of work or life.

Since 2013, the CPC has made implementing the eight-point code and practicing the mass line as the focus of work at the central, local and grass-roots levels, which produced notable effects. Reports from China Cuisine Association showed that the high-end hotels in Beijing have experienced a 35% decline in businesses following the launch of the eight-point code. According to data released by the statistical bureau, the retail sales of consumer goods from January to February 2013 totaled only RMB 3.78 trillion, up 12.3% year-on-year and down two percentage points from the growth in December 2012, a result of the declines in high-end catering and wine consumption. Commissions for discipline inspection of the CPC at both central and local levels have irregularly reported typical violations against the eight-point code to sound the alarm for other Party members. The Commission for Discipline Inspection of the CPC Shaanxi Provincial Committee alone dispatched more than 50 cadres within one month to organize 13 investigation groups and work in 12 municipalities (districts). They visited over 1,000 cadres and people in 40-plus municipalities and counties, 60-plus towns and townships (streets) and 100-plus villages (communities), hearing reports, holding talks, conducting field investigations and consulting materials. As the campaign intensifies, the formalism, bureaucracy, hedonism and extravagancy that have affected the image of the CPC as a ruling Party for a long time have been significantly reversed, and the ideological consensus of governance for the people has been rooted into the practical actions of the whole Party.

Besides proceeding from the interests of the people to correct all the unhealthy practices that may affect the relations between the Party and the masses, the CPC also pays great attention to the wisdom and role of the people in governance, and particularly respects the pioneering spirit of the people and secures their creative exploration. This is because in the view of the CPC, the masses are the real heroes who create the world and build the country and no work can be advanced without the participation of the masses.

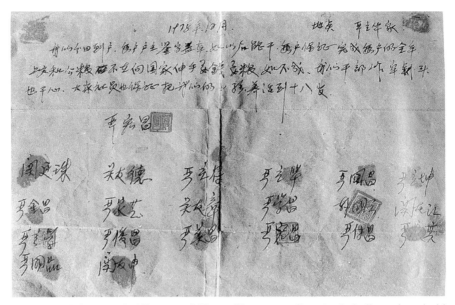

In 1978, 18 farmers in Xiaogang Village (Fengyang County, Anhui) made a bold decision to be the pioneers to put a red fingerprint on the "secret contract" to parcel out the farmland to individual households to carry out the all-round contract system.

In fact, China's reform and opening-up began with the spontaneous exploration by the masses. On November 24, 1978, 18 rural households in Xiaogang Village, Fengyang County, Anhui Province made a bold decision that might send them to jail, i.e. "contracting fields and fixing farm output quotas on the household basis". They prepared for the worst, and felt they would have nothing to regret even if the act would cost their lives in case of failure. Almost at the same time, Wu Renbao, a peasant in Huaxi Village, Jiangsu Province, began his "underground reform practice" by secretly setting up a small hardware factory together with his fellow villagers in an age when grain production was taken as the key task. In 1980, Xiangyang Town, Guanghan, Sichuan Province saw the first removal of the label of people's communes in China, with all the former enterprises reorganized into "industrial companies" and the system of "no

Under the leadership of Wu Renbao, Huaxi Village (Jiangyin, Jiangsu), which used to be a poverty-stricken village, has become the No.1 Village well-known home and abroad.

separation between governments and enterprises" was broken. In February 1980, 85 rural households in Hezhai Village, Yishan County, Guangxi voted by secret ballot and set up the first villagers' committee in China. To their surprise, all the attempts gained positive recognition and great support from leaders at both the central and local levels in a timely manner, and were improved and enriched as part of China's basic economic system and policies to guide reform and innovation in a wider scope.

China's reform enters a deep-water zone in the 21st century, when the CPC is more aware of the fact that only by giving further play to the creativity of the masses and fully mobilizing all the positive factors can it smoothly take China's reform to a new stage. In his speech at a meeting in celebration of the complete success of Shenzhou-7 manned space flight in 2008, Hu Jintao seriously noted the efforts to advocate the style of reform and innovation characterized by boldness in innovation and competition, integrity and cooperation and tolerance for failures in the whole society. During his visit to Guangdong in 2012, Xi Jinping stressed that "we shall respect the pioneering spirit of the people, propose top-level design and overall plans aimed to deepen the reform in an all-round way on the basis of in-depth investigations and researches, and shall respect practices and creation, encourage bold exploration and pool all the positive energies in relevant reforms." Under the guidance of the spirit, governments at all the levels insist on consulting the people on governance, learning about their needs and seeking their advice, establish various new platforms to collect public opinions and summarize public experience, and keep leaders and cadres in touch with the masses through Internet and mobile phone terminals to truly realize "governance relying on the people".

Scientific, Democratic and Legal Governance

While upholding the principle of "exercising overall leadership and coordinating the efforts of all parties" and the philosophy of "governance for the people and relying on the people", the CPC has deepened its understanding towards "how to govern the country well" with the advance of governance practices in the 21st century. In September 2004, the fourth plenary session of the 16th Central Committee of the CPC passed the *Decision of the CPC Central Committee on Strengthening Construction of the Party's Governance Capability*, which proposed that the whole Party must adhere to scientific, democratic and law-based governance, and keep improving the styles of leadership and governance.

For scientific governance, the CPC shall consistently explore and observe the rules for governance, socialist construction and development of the human society in combination with China's actual situations, and organize and lead the Chinese people to build the socialism with Chinese characteristics with scientific theories, scientific ideas, scientific systems and scientific approaches. To realize scientific governance, the CPC shall develop and implement its theories, lines, guidelines and policies in a scientific manner, and deploy and carry out various governance activities in a scientific manner.

To understand governance rules and establish scientific theories and ideology for governance, the CPC has always attached importance to summarizing and drawing governance experience in its own country and other countries. As early as the 1950s, Mao Zedong noted in his article entitled *On Ten Major Relations* that "we shall learn the strengths of all the nationalities and all the countries." After the launch of China's reform and opening-up,

The local government of Wannian County of Jiangxi adopted effective service mechanism featuring an accountability system concerning related leaders and departments and support by cadres to guarantee the connections between the grassroots and the mass. The picture shows two cadres from the government of the Suqiao Township of Wannian County are talking with the farmers at the edge of the farmland to learn about the conditions of agricultural production.

Deng Xiaoping often told the whole Party to draw all the advanced ways of management that reflect rules of modern production across the world, including developed capitalist countries. To push forward the construction of the socialism with Chinese characteristics, Jiang Zemin repeatedly required that "a clear idea must be established that all the civilization that is positive and advanced shall be learnt and applied, no matter under which social system it is created." In the 21st century, Hu Jintao expressed the idea in a clearer manner, emphasizing "the ability to combine excellent traditions in Chinese culture with advanced civilizations of foreign countries". Xi Jinping further noted the efforts to study and draw the experience of capitalist economies and positive governance experience of other countries by proceeding from China's reality. It can be seen that the CPC is working to broaden its horizon and mind to better master the rules for construction of governance capability amid the changes in world political and economic landscape and develop the governance theories and ideology that are adaptive to China's actual situations.

Besides establishing and developing scientific theories and ideology, scientific decision-making is the key to scientific governance. As early as the 14th National Congress of the CPC, Jiang Zemin proposed the idea of "accelerating establishment of a democratic and scientific system for decision-making", and required "organs and leaders to earnestly hear public opinions, give full play to the role of experts and research consulting agencies and quickly put in place a set of decision-making systems that are scientific and democratic." As the understanding for scientific decision-making goes deeper, the 16th National Congress of the CPC imposed clear requirements on the reform in intra-Party decision-making mechanism in its report, noting "correct decisions are important preconditions for the success of various work, and efforts shall be made to improve the decision-making mechanism that allows deeper understanding for the conditions of the people, fully reflects public wills, extensively pools public wisdom and actually cherishes public forces, and to make decision-making more scientific and democratic. Decision-making organs at all levels must improve the rules and procedures for making major decisions, establish the system for feedback of social conditions and public feelings, and put in place the system for publicity of major issues and the system for public hearings that are closely related to public interests; They shall enhance expert consulting systems, implement the argumentation system and accountability system for decision-making and avoid arbitrary decision-making."

The CPC made great efforts in improving decision-making mechanisms in recent years. On one hand, it puts in place the systems for major policy negotiation and opinion solicitation, frequently holding negotiations, talks and briefings among non-party personages to hear opinions and suggestions, and

On December 2, 2013, the Ministry of Environmental Protection of the People's Republic of China held the hearing on the administrative approval to the environmental impact assessment documents concerning the project of the special railway line between Beijing and Shenyang.

soliciting opinions in various regions and departments about major meeting topics, documents and affairs at central and local levels. On the other hand, both central and local organs generally establish meeting systems and working rules, clearly defining the scope, principles, procedures and disciplines of meetings; Some local organs publicize the affairs closely related to people's interests and hold corresponding hearings, while introducing the resignation system for the cadres who made wrong decisions. To make scientific decisions actually implemented in governance activities, the CPC would regulate detailed procedures and requirements for implementation once a decision is made, and ensure the decision to be in charge and funded through the cadre responsibility system and some other systems; The CPC also highlights comprehensive evaluation of implementation of decisions, adjusts guidelines and policies in a timely manner during evaluation and strictly implements reward and punishment measures after the evaluation.

On June 26, 2003, the Party committee and government of Songmen Town of Wenling of Zhejiang held the 14th democratic meeting to collect opinions for the best solution for the adjustment of the school network.

For democratic governance, the CPC shall develop the socialist democratic politics with Chinese characteristics, make the socialist democratic politics increasingly institutionalized, regulated and procedure-based, and ensure that the people are masters of the country with democratic systems, democratic forms and democratic means. Developing socialist democratic politics has always been the goal of the CPC. As early as the period of Chinese Revolutionary War, the CPC represented by Mao Zedong had fruitful exploration in establishing the people's political power and developing democratic politics and accumulated rich experience. After the founding of the New China, the people's democratic dictatorship was made as the state system and the people's congress system as the form of government, and the system of multi-party cooperation and political consultation under the leadership of the CPC and the system of regional autonomy were introduced. These great practices laid the foundation for China's political construction and development of political civilization, and became an important institutional base for the CPC to realize democratic governance. Over the past three decades since China's reform and opening-up, particularly entering the 21st century, the CPC has been dedicated to consolidating and developing the said three fundamental systems to advance the orderly development of China's democracy. Meanwhile, with the growing room for autonomy in China's society, the CPC has also kept expanding democracy at the grassroots level, giving play to the positive role of grassroots organizations in safeguarding public interests, reflecting public appeals, managing grassroots affairs and promoting public participation, strengthening the autonomous function of grassroots organizations of various kinds and expanding the channels for grassroots masses to exercise self-management, self-services, self-education and self-supervision, in an effort to perfectly combine government administration with grassroots democracy.

Efforts have been made to promote the people's democracy with intra-Party democracy. As a ruling Party, the CPC dominates the political progress of the whole country. This determines that the development of intra-Party democracy directly shapes that of the people's democracy. Specifically speaking, the awareness, involvement and abilities of Party members in political affairs directly affect the people's enthusiasm for and ability in political participation; How the intra-Party political activities are institutionalized, regulated and procedure-based determines the level of political activities in the whole country; The growth and expansion of intra-Party democratic elements promote the progress of the people's democracy. Therefore, the CPC has vigorously encouraged its Party members and cadres to bring the democratic awareness, styles and habits developed in intra-Party activities into the activities of State organs at all levels and of the society, thus effectively promoting the overall development of the socialist democracy.

To practice democratic governance, the CPC has consistently expanded democracy in cadre personnel work. On one hand, it has put in place scientific

On November 2, 2011, grassroots Party representatives of Guang'an (Sichuan) are voting for the members and alternate members of the Municipal Commission for Discipline Inspection.

systems for cadre selection, appointment, supervision and management. In 2002, the CPC Central Committee released the *Regulations for Selection and Appointment of Party and Government Cadres*, which offered comprehensive provisions for every part of the work related to selection and appointment of cadres. In 2004, the General Office of the CPC Central Committee further promulgated the *Interim Regulations for Public Selection of Party and Government Cadres and the Interim Regulations for Competition for Leading Posts in Party and Government Organs*, which clearly defined the application scope, selection procedures, test & inspection methods, disciplines and supervision for open selection and competition for leading posts, and advanced the normalization and institutionalization of the work. On the other hand, it has improved the democratic decision-making mechanism for selection and appointment of cadres in Party committees. Based on summarization of experience, the CPC Central Committee released the *Measures for Voting by*

On March 28, 2014, a total of 45 Party members from the Party and government organizations of the Nanchansi Subdistrict of Wuxi visited the Wuxi Duty Crime Prevention and Warning Education Base.

the Plenary Meeting of the Party's Local Committees for Candidates Proposed or Recommended to Principal Leaders in Party Committees and Governments at a Lower Level, which explicitly specified that the candidates proposed or recommended to be the principal leaders of Party committees and governments at the municipal and county levels generally shall be nominated by the standing committee of the Party committee at a higher level and further submitted to the plenary meetings for voting by secret ballot; In case of the need for urgent appointment during the inter-session period of plenary meetings, the opinions of members of the plenary meetings shall be solicited. In addition, the *Civil Servant Law of the People's Republic of China* reviewed and passed by the NPC in April 2005 was also a major move intended to make cadre personnel work more scientific, democratic and institutionalized, and was of great significance to implementing the strategy of running the country according to law and advancing construction of the socialist democratic politics.

For law-based governance, the CPC shall adhere to the basic strategy of running the country according to law, lead the people to develop laws, take the lead to observe laws and adopt measures to secure implementation of laws. The purpose is to make the country's economic, political, cultural and social activities increasingly legalized and regulated, and to ensure effective governance of the country by the people under the leadership of the Party with the philosophy, systems and procedures for law-based governance.

As early as the Warring States Period in ancient China, some politicians proposed the idea that "a state would become chaotic if not ruled by law". From the 1950s to the early 1980s, the CPC did not fundamentally establish the philosophy of governing the country by law and mainly governed the country with policies, although it led the country to develop laws and regulations. If governance by policies is defined as "politics" different from the common concept, the effects of such "politics" rely on the abilities of those making and executing the policies. Obviously, "politics" is a form of the rule by man, as policies are subjective, arbitrary and easily changed. Policies of the CPC were once considered changeable. By contrast, laws are more rigid. Once formulated, laws cannot be changed arbitrarily, and generally include detailed provisions. No crime without law making it so. With laws, bigger room of explanation is offered for judgment of whether policies are abided by.

After China's reform and opening-up, Deng Xiaoping, when summarizing the lessons from the "cultural revolution", noted that "the problem was laws were not complete and many remained absent. Words of leaders were typically regarded as the 'law' and opposing what leaders said was 'violation' against the law. 'Laws' varied with words of leaders." In 1980, he warned the whole Party that efforts should be made to consolidate and develop the political situation characterized by stability and solidarity and effectively fight all the forces that endanger the stability and solidarity. Instead of launching political campaigns in the past, the principles of the socialist legal system must be observed. Afterwards, the CPC began to establish and improve the country's legal system, while advocating to "act in strict accordance with the law" by all the Party members and cadres as well as people of all social strata. In 1997, the CPC Central Committee proposed the ideology of "improving the socialist legal system, governing the country by law and building China into a socialist country under the rule of law". "Governing the country by law" became the basic strategy for the CPC to govern the country.

In the view of the CPC, governing the country by law means the masses, under the leadership of the Party, manage economic, cultural and social affairs in accordance with the Constitution and laws and through various means and forms, so as to ensure advance of every work according to law and gradually realize the institutionalization and legalization of socialist democracy, in which the institutions and laws will not change with the changes in leadership or with the ideas and focuses of leaders. Law-based governance is the core part

On December 2, 2012, the Department of Justice of the Shuanghe Subdistrict Office of Huaying (Sichuan) held the knowledge contest on the *Constitution*.

of implementing the strategy of governing the country by law. That is, when operating the State power, the CPC cannot overstep the Constitution or laws for its leading position. Therefore, the CPC has always worked to intensify implementation of the Constitution and laws during the process of governance, defend the unity, dignity and authority of the socialist legal system and create the legal environment in which the people are not willing or able to and do not dare to break the laws, so as to ensure that there are laws to abide by, the laws are observed and strictly enforced. As required by the CPC Central Committee, administrative organs at all levels, as the major subject to implement laws and regulations, must take the lead to strictly enforce the laws and safeguard public interests, the people's interests and social orders; Leading organs and cadres at all levels must keep improving their abilities to apply the thinking and approaches of governance by law, and work to develop consensuses on reforms, regulate

The organization department of the CPC Chun'an Committee has been paying high attention to the self-development of the cadres engaged in the work related to organization. On February 7, 2014, the first working day after the Spring Festival, the organization department provided a training for the cadres to learn about the newly amended *Regulations on the Work of Selecting and Appointing Leading Cadres of Party and Government*, which was ended with a closed-book examination.

development behaviors, resolve contradictions and secure social harmony through law-based governance. The philosophy and practices about law-based governance and governing the country by law provide the base of legitimacy for the ruling position of the CPC and help the CPC exercise its right to governance in an all-round way within the institutional framework of the State power.

Self-building

After 90 years of efforts, the CPC has evolved from a party that led the people in the struggle for state power to a party that has led the people in exercising the power and has long been remained in power; It has developed from a party that led national reconstruction under external blockade and a planned economy to a party that is leading national development while the country is opening to the outside world and developing a socialist market economy; It has grown from a small party that had only tens of members when it was first founded to a big party that presently has more than 80 million members and sees significant changes in the member and cadre teams. Amid the constant changes in the global, national and intra-Party conditions, it has attached great importance to its own construction to maintain its advanced nature and purity.

General Setup for the Construction of the Party

The CPC regards its own construction as a "magic weapon" by which it has led revolution, construction and reform to constant victories. The Party's construction resembles a systematic and great project. To achieve victories one after another, the CPC must adjust and make the overall deployment for its construction based on the changes in its historical positioning and central tasks in different periods, providing the construction practices with clear guidance and ensuring that the Party has always walked in the forefront of the historical progress despite drastic changes in world situations, has always been the mainstay of the Chinese people in the response to all the risks and challenges

On December 24, 2013, the docent was giving an explanation on the exhibits at the large-scale exhibition tour themed on "understanding the laws based on the cases and combating corruption and building a clean government".

both at home and abroad, and has always been the strong core of leadership during the development of socialism with Chinese characteristics.

As early as the fifth plenary session of the 11th Central Committee of the CPC held in February 1980, Deng Xiaoping explicitly proposed the need to answer the question of "what shall a ruling party be like". At the second plenary session of the 12th Central Committee of the CPC held in 1983, Deng Xiaoping further pointed out that "efforts shall be made to build the CPC into a Marxist political party with strong combat power and the strong core that leads the Chinese people in the construction of socialist material civilization and spiritual civilization." This clearly defines the goals for the Party's construction in the new period. As China presses ahead its reform and opening-up, the CPC has kept enriching the meanings of the goals for the Party's construction. In 1994, the fourth plenary session of the 14th Central Committee of the CPC put forward the general goal for the new great project of the Party's construction. In 1997, the 15th National Congress of the CPC described the general goal in a more comprehensive and accurate manner, which was to "make the Party a Marxist political party that is armed with Deng Xiaoping Theory, that serves the people wholeheartedly, that is completely consolidated ideologically, politically and organizationally, that can withstand all trials and tribulations, that is always at the forefront of the times and that leads the people of the country in building socialism with Chinese characteristics."

In the 21st century, the Central Committee of the CPC put forward the Important Thought of "Three Represents", providing ideas for further specifying the "overall deployment of the Party's construction". In his speech marking the 80th anniversary of the founding of the CPC delivered on July 1, 2001, Jiang Zemin proposed the Party's historic direction and two major historic issues facing the Party for the first time, and pointed out that "the Party has evolved from a party that led the people in the struggle for state power to a party that has led the people in exercising the power and has long been remained in power, and has developed from a party that led national reconstruction under external blockade and a planned economy to a party that is leading national development while the country is opening to the outside world and developing a socialist market economy." Therefore, the CPC must "further address the two historic issues, i.e. how to improve the Party's ruling ability and leadership and how to enhance its ability to resist against corruption and risks." This highlighted the fundamental features about ruling. In 2002, the 16th National Congress of the CPC presented the key issue about "strengthening the Party's ruling ability construction" and summarized five major ruling abilities for the first time. In fact, this initially identified the main position of ruling in the overall deployment of the Party's construction. The fourth plenary session of the 16th Central Committee of the CPC held in September 2004 passed the *Decision of the Central Committee*

On March 12, 2005, the CPC members and cadres joined the education activity aimed to "maintain the advanced nature of the CPC members" and "practice the important thought of 'Three Represents'" at Xibaipo, Hebei Province, a sacred place of the Chinese revolution. The photo shows the CPC members sign their names on the Party flag.

of the CPC on Strengthening the Party's Ruling Ability Construction, which summarized the main ruling experience of the Party over the past 55 years, outlined the basic meanings of the Party's ruling ability, specified the guidelines, general goals and main tasks and initially established the framework for the Party's ruling ability construction.

In the 21st century, the Central Committee of the CPC has strengthened the Party's construction in the spirit of reform and innovation, and continued to explore the way to make overall deployment. In his speech delivered at the fifth plenary session of the 16th Central Committee of the CPC held in October 2005, Hu Jintao explicitly pointed out that "the CPC will focus on further development of its ruling ability and advanced nature and advance its ideological, organizational, work-style and institutional construction." In his speech made at the 85th anniversary of the founding of the CPC in 2006, Hu summarized the experience gained in the nationwide education campaign aimed to maintain the advanced nature of the Party members, and took construction of the Party's advanced nature to a higher level that concerns the success of the socialist construction in China and the destiny of the CPC. It can be seen that enhancing the Party's ruling ability and maintaining its advanced nature are the two core goals of the CPC in its efforts to intensify construction in the 21st century. During the practice of maintaining its advanced nature, the CPC increasingly recognizes that purity is a must for maintaining its advanced nature as it's a key reflection of the latter amid the new situations. In his address to the seventh plenary session of the 17th Central Committee of the CPC held in early 2012, Hu Jintao highlighted the importance of maintaining the Party's purity against the new backdrop. At the 18th National Congress of the CPC also held in 2012, he further stated that to advance the new great work of the Party's construction in an all-round way, "efforts must be made to tightly seize the main theme of intensifying the Party's ruling ability construction as well as the construction of its advanced nature and purity." The CPC thus had identified the theme for its construction.

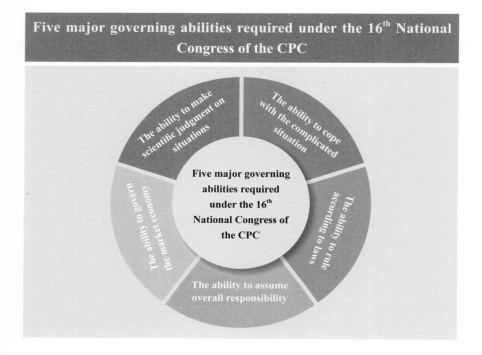

Five major governing abilities required under the 16th National Congress of the CPC

The ability to make scientific judgment on situations

The ability to cope with the complicated situation

The ability to govern the market economy

Five major governing abilities required under the 16th National Congress of the CPC

The ability to rule according to laws

The ability to assume overall responsibility

Guided by the theme, the CPC divides its construction into five parts and specified respective focuses: Ideologically, it will focus on fortifying the convictions of Party members; Organizationally, it will put emphasis on bringing up the qualification of the Party members and cadres; In improving the Party's style of work, it will stress the maintenance of its close ties with the people; Institutionally, it will emphasize improving democratic centralism; In enhancing the Party's capacity to fight corruption and uphold integrity, it will focus on improving the systems for punishing and preventing corruption. All this covers every aspect of the Party's construction, with the ultimate goal of building the CPC into a learning, service and innovation-oriented Marxist ruling party and ensuring that the CPC is always the strong core of leadership in the socialist construction with Chinese characteristics.

It can be concluded that through 30-plus years of exploration since China's reform and opening-up, the CPC has had relatively complete understanding towards the "overall deployment of the Party's construction" and comprehensively answered the key question of "what kind of Party to build and how to build", which charters the course for the Party's construction amid new situations. During concrete implementation, the CPC works to build itself into a more scientific way in the spirit of being on guard against adversity in times of peace and forging boldly ahead.

Pay Attention to Theoretical Innovation and Be Armed with Theory

In the view of the CPC, self-management is a must for maintaining its vitality and consolidating its ruling position. The first step towards self-management is to intensify education for Party members, particularly leaders and cadres, so as to make them fully embrace the guiding ideology, routes, principles and policies of the Party, develop all the merits necessary for Party members and the morality necessary for being officials and engaged in politics, enhance the awareness of law and the Party's disciplines and establish common political will and value orientation. This is crucial to a political party, and is the adhesive that bonds all the members of a political organization. The key to winning the recognition of all is that the Party's theories are capable of answering the new questions arising from the practices in different periods and offering scientific guidance to the practices. Therefore, the CPC has never adhered to old theories, but paid great importance to theoretical innovation and consistently injected new life into Marxism.

After the founding of the New China, with the fundamental completion of China's socialist transformation and the kickoff of constructing the socialist cause in an all-round way, the Party's first generation of central collective leadership with Comrade Mao Zedong at the core proposed that the CPC should combine Marxism with China's actual situations for the second time during the socialist revolution and construction period, so as to find the correct path for China, and described a number of useful propositions related to the construction, such as the "Four Modernizations", during the process of exploration. After the third plenary session of the 11th Central Committee of the CPC, the second generation of central collective leadership with Comrade Deng Xiaoping at the core shifted the focus of work for the CPC and China to economic construction, launching reform and opening-up. During the great practice of leading the CPC and the Chinese people in carrying out socialist construction, the second generation of central collective leadership developed Deng Xiaoping Theory, formulated the basic line, i.e. keeping economic development as the central task, persevering in reform and opening up and adhering to the Four Cardinal Principles, blazed a new path to the socialist construction with Chinese characteristics, and systematically and preliminarily answered a series of basic questions as to how to build, consolidate and develop socialism in a country like China that is less developed economically and culturally; It defended the socialist system and took China on the fast track of development in the critical period that featured drastic changes in international landscape.

In the 21st century, the world has seen multi-polarization and economic globalization evolving amid twists and turns, scientific & technological progresses constantly changing and competition about overall national strength

The mass parade raised the slogan of "Upholding Deng Xiaoping Theory" at the ceremony to celebrate the 60th anniversary of the founding of the New China in Beijing on October 1, 2009.

increasingly intense. Politicians in major countries proceeded from their own national interests and considered their goals and prospects in the new century. Against the backdrop, the third generation of central collective leadership with Comrade Jiang Zemin at the core raised the important thought of "Three Represents", that is, the CPC must always represent the development trend of China's advanced productive forces, the orientation of China's advanced culture and the fundamental interests of the overwhelming majority of the Chinese people; It led the CPC and the Chinese people in defending and developing the socialist cause with Chinese characteristics, and successfully pushed it into the 21st century.

After three decades of practice, China's reform has ushered into a stage where critical problems need to be addressed and various contradictions get increasingly prominent, which requires the CPC to further answer the major theoretical and practical question of "what is development, and why and how to develop". Therefore, the fourth generation of central collective leadership with Comrade Hu Jintao at the core began to explore the way for development with Chinese characteristics right after the generation was formed. The third plenary session of the 16th Central Committee of the CPC held in Beijing in October 2003 gave a complete description about the scientific outlook on development for the first time, and proposed to "still put people first, establish a comprehensive, coordinated and sustainable outlook on development, and promote the all-round development of economy, society and humans." Based on the summary of practical experience, the 17th National Congress of the CPC held in 2007 systematically interpreted the spiritual essence and fundamental requirements of the scientific outlook on development. In 2012, the report of the 18th National Congress of the CPC put the scientific outlook on development on the list of the guiding ideology that the CPC must adhere to for a long time together with Marxism-Leninism, Mao Zedong Thought and Deng Xiaoping Theory and the Important Thought of Three Represents, once again keeping the Party's ideology updated with the time. The report also comprehensively described the basic

In February 2000, Jiang Zemin delivered an important speech at the Educational Conference on Study, Political Awareness and Integrity of the Leading Cadres of Gaozhou, Guangdong, and first put forward the Three Represents thought.

connotation and inherent relations as well as the general basis, deployment and missions of the socialism with Chinese characteristics, systematically enriched the system of theories of socialism with Chinese characteristics, and thus chartered the course for China's future development.

While the Party's leadership actively considers the important issues concerning China's development, the CPC also gives play to the role of theory workers and encourages them contribute to the Party's theoretical innovation. In 2004, the Central Committee of the CPC initiated the national project to study and develop Marxist theory, organizing 24 main project teams and base project teams, designating chief experts and key members of the project teams and setting up the project consulting committee. Researchers made Deng Xiaoping Theory, the Important Thought of "Three Represents" and the scientific outlook on development as the focus of the research and set key realistic issues as the direction of efforts, and highlighted the work in five aspects: First, strengthening research on the innovation to Marxism based on China's actual situations and major realistic issues; Second, intensifying the compilation and translation of and research on classical works about Marxism; Third, establishing the Marxist theoretical base as well as the philosophy and social science systems with characteristics of the time; Fourth, compiling teaching materials for key disciplines, including philosophy, political economics, scientific socialism, politics, sociology, law, history, journalism and literature, that reflect the latest theoretical achievements of Marxism in contemporary China, and developing the teaching material system for philosophy and social science; Fifth, building a backbone team that consists of old, middle and young members for Marxism research and teaching. After implementation of the project, more than 100 seminars of various kinds were held, and nearly 5,000 theoretical essays were published in major newspapers and magazines of the Central Committee of the CPC. Key works of Marx, Engels and Lenin were re-translated and revised, and

Student Party members from Nanjing University of Aeronautics and Astronautics and retired Party members from Baida District (Nanjing) were exchanging views on learning and practicing the scientific outlook on development.

10 volumes of Karl Marx and Frederick Engels and five volumes of the Collected Works of Lenin were edited and published. The Marxist discipline system was also established in schools of higher learning, which greatly pushed forward the construction of the talent team studying Marxist theories.

In the view of the CPC, only absorbed by the brains can the theoretical innovation be transferred into strong spiritual power and conscious actions of the Party members and cadres, and be further used to guide practice and advance the cause of the Party and the Chinese people from one victory to another. That's why the CPC has worked to arm the brains of all its members, especially leading cadres, with the latest Marxist achievements with Chinese characteristics, unleashed a new surge of learning and implementing Deng Xiaoping Theory and the Important Thought of "Three Represents" within the whole Party, launched the education campaign aimed to maintain the advanced nature of the Party members and carried out activities to deepen the practice related to the scientific outlook on development since the reform and opening-up, particularly the 21st century. While advancing the large-scale learning campaign, the Central Committee of the CPC increasingly recognizes that cultivating the awareness of conscious learning among all the Party members and transferring theoretical innovation into the active behaviors of all the Party members are of particular importance. This is also the aim and core of the CPC in its proposal to build itself a learning-oriented Marxist political party.

In September 2009, the fourth plenary session of the 17th Central Committee of the CPC passed the *Decision on Major Issues Concerning Strengthening and Improving Party Construction under the New Situation*, warning all the Party members that consistently learning, being good at learning, and working to master and apply the new ideologies, knowledge and experience of all the scientific disciplines is decisive for the Party to stay in the forefront of the time and lead China's development as the world is changing and the practices of building socialism with Chinese characteristics will go further. The CPC must focus its efforts on building itself into a learning-oriented Marxist political party and regard it as a major and pressing strategic task by arming all the Party members with scientific theories, embracing a global vision, seizing objective rules and developing innovation spirits. In December 2009, the General Office of the CPC Central Committee released the *Opinions on Advancing Construction of Learning-oriented Party Organizations*, which overviewed the significance, general requirements, key principles, main contents and approaches of building learning-oriented Party organizations. Afterwards, the Party organizations at all levels worked to create the atmosphere in which every Party member highlights, advocates and persists in learning, gradually established the philosophy about lifetime learning by all, and put in place effective learning systems. All these helped the Party members constantly increase their learning abilities and knowledge and play their vanguard and exemplary role, and helped the Party

On May 7, 2014, the first "family Party school", namely the Bayi Community Family Party School, was established at the community at South Qingnian Road, Donghe District, Hami, Xinjiang. The picture shows 12 Party members from different ethnic groups are attending the class at the school.

organizations strengthen their creativity, cohesiveness and capability.

Traditional learning focuses on absorption of knowledge and information, while learning-oriented Party organizations stress transformation of ways of thinking, and highlight the main role of Party members, encouraging them to break away from old thought patterns and make bold innovation. Surely, the purpose is to pool the wisdom of all the Party members and better answer the questions that the CPC encounters in the construction of socialism with Chinese characteristics, such as how to make all the Party members stay firm in their conviction, how to tackle various circumstances and problems arising from China's reform process, how to guide the Chinese society in the forefront of the times, and how to maintain the advanced nature of the CPC amid the new situations to avoid degeneration and corruption.

Set Up and Improve the Party's Institutional System

Institutional civilization is a key part of human civilization. Institutions are the rules and codes of conduct for all the members of a political party and reflect the common will and interests of the whole party. Whether the systems and mechanisms are scientific largely determines the ruling ability of a ruling party. It's inconceivable if the CPC, a ruling party that has more than 80 million members, over three million grassroots organizations and numerous middle and high-level organizations, has not put in place a full set of intra-Party institutional system based on the Party constitution.

On November 9, 2012, the press center of the 18th National Congress of the CPC held the first news conference and, Wang Jingqing, vice minister of the Organization Department of the CPC Central Committee, made an introduction to the Party building and answered the questions of the reporters.

However, the Central Committee of the CPC didn't pay enough attention to institutional construction, but focused on construction of ideology, organization and work style during a relatively long period after the founding of the New China. After the end of the 10-year "cultural revolution", the second generation of central collective leadership with Comrade Deng Xiaoping at the core began to realize the importance of building the Party with institutions. In the early years of China's reform, Deng Xiaoping, while putting emphasis on transforming the Party's ideological and political lines, explicitly pointed out the path for construction of intra-Party statutes and placed the reform at a key position to the leadership institutions of the Party and the country, including cadre systems, mass supervision and discipline inspection. He stressed that the laws of the Party is the guarantee of the national laws, and put forward brand-new ideas and overall thoughts, including launching the reform to the Party's leadership system, improving the Party's regulations and laws, making intra-Party activities

On December 1, 2012, Shanghai Entry-Exit Inspection and Quarantine Bureau and China Executive Leadership Academy (Pudong) signed the cooperation agreement and held the inauguration ceremony for the education station for scientific Party building in organizations.

democratic and institutional, and governing and building the Party with the Party's legal system. This greatly enriched the theories about the Party's construction, and the new ideas and ways of thinking in construction of intra-Party statutes had particularly significant influence on intra-Party activities.

After 1990s, the CPC took its institutional construction into a fast track, releasing a package of intra-Party statutes and regulatory documents and initially establishing the intra-Party institutional system. But with the profound changes in the global, national and intra-Party conditions, problems related to the disconnection and inconsistency of intra-Party legal systems became increasingly prominent. In particular, some intra-Party statutes and regulatory documents lagged behind the needs of practice and actual situations; Some were inconsistent with the Party constitution, the Party's theories, guidelines and policies and even China's Constitution and laws; Some overlapped or conflicted with each other, greatly hindering the effective play of the binding role of the intra-Party system. In the 21st century, intra-Party institutional construction ushers into a forward-looking and scientific path. By pressing precaution ahead and extending punishment and by seizing preemptive opportunities and making

On July 6, 2012, the lecture themed on "cultural charm and clean governance" was held in the exhibition hall of the Zhaobo Anti-corruption Education Base (Yiyang, Henan). All seats were occupied.

active preparation, intra-Party statutes have improved in every aspect ranging from legislation, enforcement to observance and maintenance. In 2009, the fourth plenary session of the 17th Central Committee of the CPC stressed efforts to intensify intra-Party institutional innovation and put in place an institutional system with the Party constitution as the foundation and with democratic centralism as the core, with the aim to build the Party into a more scientific, institutional and regulated way, develop intra-Party democracy, ensure the unity of the Party and boost the vigor of the Party in creation. In May 2013, the Central Committee of the CPC released the *Rules of the CPC for Formulating Intra-Party Statutes*, which explicitly specified the authority and principles for developing intra-Party statutes as well as planning, drafting, approval, release, application, interpretation, filing, clearance and assessment.

So far, the CPC has put in place a systematic intra-Party legal system. In particular, the Party Constitution is the fundamental intra-Party law and the basis for developing other Intra-Party statutes, as it's about the fundamental provisions of the Party's nature and aim, lines and program, guiding ideology and goals, organizational principles and structure, Party members' obligations and rights as well as the Party's discipline. Intra-Party statutes have six levels under the Party Constitution: Codes, regulations, rules, provisions, measures and detailed rules. Among them, codes include fundamental provisions about the Party's political activities, organizational activities and the behaviors of all the Party members, such as the *Numerous Codes for Clean Governance by the CPC Members and Cadres*; Regulations specify comprehensive provisions about important relations in a certain field or important work in a certain aspect of the Party, such as the *Regulations for Guaranteeing the Rights of the CPC Members*; Rules, provisions, measures and detailed rules are about the concrete provisions regarding the important work or items in a certain aspect of the Party, such as the *Interim Provision on Implementing Accountability of CPC and Government Leaders and Cadres*, the *Implementation Measures for Numerous Provisions Concerning Honesty and Self-discipline of Leaders in Central Enterprises (Trial) and the*

Detailed Rules of the Regulations for Case Inspection by the Discipline Authority of the CPC.

To further regulate intra-Party institutional construction and ensure sound operation of intra-Party systems, the Central Committee of the CPC deployed and carried out the work related to centralized clearance of intra-Party statutes and regulatory documents in 2012, which was the first time in the history of the CPC. It is a fundamental work for the Party's institutional construction, and is of far-reaching significance to comprehensively learning about intra-Party institutions, effectively maintaining the harmony and consistency of intra-Party statutes, accelerating construction of intra-Party legal systems and actually improving the scientific level of the Party's construction. The whole work was carried out in two phases: Phase I (July 2012-September 2013), in which intra-Party statutes and regulatory documents developed between 1978 and June 2012 were sorted out; Phase II (October 2013-December 2014), in which intra-Party statutes and regulatory documents developed before 1978 were sorted out. During Phase I, the General Office of the Central Committee of the CPC, in collaboration with

The procurators at the Procuratorate of Sheqi (Henan), signed the *Letter of Commitment to Clean Governance* on January 12, 2012.

relevant authorities, sorted out 767 intra-Party statutes and regulatory documents released between 1978 and June 2012, studied, demonstrated and reviewed the documents one by one and fully solicited opinions of relevant sides. On such a basis, the Central Committee of the CPC decided to abolish 162 intra-Party statutes and regulatory documents with part of the contents conflicting with the Party Constitution and the Party's theories, lines, guidelines and policies, inconsistent with the Constitution and laws, obviously not adapting to actual needs or having been covered or replaced by new regulations, and announced ineffectiveness of 138 intra-Party statutes and regulatory documents with the objects of adjustment having disappeared or the term of application having matured. The rest 467 intra-Party statutes and regulatory documents continued to be effective, and 42 of them needed revisions. According to the requirements of the Central Committee of the CPC, the Party presently embarks on organization of Phase II work, and is expected to complete the work by the end of December 2014. Meanwhile, the CPC also needs to improve the mechanism for regular and immediate clearance, and will sort out intra-Party statutes and

On March 23, 2010, at the Clean Governance Education Conference for the leading Party cadres of Changsha, Lei Yuan, former deputy mayor of Chenzhou, admonished the leading Party cadres of their responsibilities for clean governance with his own example.

regulatory documents in a centralized manner every five years in the future; While formulating or revising intra-Party statutes and regulatory documents, relevant intra-Party statutes and regulatory documents that are inconsistent or inharmonious with them shall also be cleared at the same time to make clearance more regular, institutional and regulated.

The vitality of systems lies in execution. Being fully aware of the fact, the CPC has increasingly focused on improving the power to execute systems during intra-Party institutional construction. First of all, it improves the institutional awareness of all the Party members through publicity and education. By giving lectures, launching special columns, organizing exhibitions and making analysis, it intensifies publicity and education about intra-Party systems to strengthen the institutional awareness of Party members and cadres and cement the ideological foundation for observing discipline and laws. It establishes the awareness within the Party that "everyone is equal before the law and has no privileges before systems, and institutional constraints have no exceptions", requiring leaders and cadres, particularly those who play first fiddle, to take the lead to learn systems, strictly execute systems and consciously maintaining systems. Second, it does a good job in detailing and implementing systems, actually transfers every system of the Party into the codes of conduct for all the Party members and cadres, and develops a truly sound atmosphere within the Party in which everyone is disciplined by systems and does everything according to regulations. Third, it highlights supervision and inspection and strengthens effects of execution. Discipline inspection and supervision authorities at various levels inspect the implementation of the systems, awarding the organizations and individuals that well execute the systems and punishing those that execute the systems poorly; They keep improving system accountability and execution, make system implementation part of the annual assessment for organizations or individuals, and link assessment results with promotion and appraisal of cadres.

Continuously Improve the Party's Style of Work

The Party's work style is a unique concept for the theories of a Marxist political party. It reflects the Party's nature and world outlook in the Party's work and activities, and the consistent attitudes and behaviors of the whole Party, including the Party's organizations and individual members at various levels, in politics, ideology, organization, work, life and other aspects that reflect the Party's nature and principles. In the view of a Marxist political party, the most direct and easiest way for the mass to know a political party is to observe its work style. Therefore, the CPC attaches great importance to the construction of the Party's work style, and considers it is concerned with the Party's image, popularity and destiny.

Xibaipo, a sacred place for the Chinese revolution.

In the early years after founding, the CPC established its nature as a proletarian vanguard and put forward the ideology about construction of work style, i.e. publicizing and organizing the mass and relying on and leading workers. The seventh National Congress of the CPC summarized the excellent work style of the Party developed during long-term struggle in three aspects, i.e. the work style of combining theories and practices, the work style of linking closely with the people and the work style of self-criticism. Afterwards, Mao Zedong warned the whole Party at the second plenary session of the seventh Central Committee of the CPC that "all the comrades must keep the work style of modesty and prudence and be free from arrogance and impetuosity, and must keep the work style of hard struggle." Always keeping in mind the said two "musts" has become a must for all the Party members in the following decades.

In the early years of China's reform and opening-up, Deng Xiaoping sharply noted that "the work style of a ruling party concerns its future destiny." After the middle 1990s, the CPC further intensified the awareness of potential crises related to ruling. In October 1996, the sixth plenary session of the 14th Central Committee of the CPC decided to carry out an education campaign about learning, politics and integrity among cadres above the county level. In November 1998, the Central Committee of the CPC released the *Opinions on Moving Deeper the Education Campaign about Learning, Politics and Integrity among CPC and Government Cadres above the County Level*, specifying requirements, steps and approaches for the campaign. Later on, the CPC and government cadres above the county level received the education in three batches from top to bottom. From December 22, 1999, the Standing Committee of the Central Committee of the CPC spent five and a half days reviewing and summarizing the practices and experience over the decade since the fourth plenary session of the 13th Central Committee of the CPC, checking the weaknesses in work and carrying out criticism and self-criticism. By the end of 2000 when the campaign was over, a total of 700,000 CPC cadres received the education, and more than five million cadres both inside and outside the CPC

On September 28, 2010, a democratic evaluation conference was held at the Hesha Town Junior Middle School by the Yongxing Working Committee of the Commission for Discipline Inspection of Chuanshan District, Suining, Sichuan.

and the mass heard the mobilization reports, participated in democratic tests and helped with the rectification.

In the 21st century, the CPC continued to push forward construction of the work style. The sixth plenary session of the 15th Central Committee of the CPC convened in 2001 held a special meeting on the construction of the Party's work style, and released the *Decision on Strengthening and Improving Construction of the Work Style of the CPC*, requiring all the Party members, especially cadres, to fulfill "eight do's and eight don'ts". (1. Emancipate the mind and seek truth from facts; do not keep doing things the old way. 2. Combine theory with practice; do not copy mechanically or worship books. 3. Keep close ties with the people; don't be formalistic or bureaucratic. 4. Adhere to the principle of democratic centralism; do not act arbitrarily or be feeble and lax. 5. Abide by Party discipline; do not pursue liberalism. 6. Be honest and upright; do not abuse power for personal gains. 7. Work hard; do not be hedonistic. 8. Appoint people on their merits; do not practice favoritism in personnel placement.) The third plenary session of the 16th Central Committee of the CPC held in October 2003 put forward that efforts must be made to intensify construction of the work style, so as to serve the people and be pragmatic and incorruptible. In his speech delivered at the seventh plenary session of the 16th Central Commission for Discipline Inspection of the CPC in 2007, Hu Jintao called for intensified efforts in comprehensive construction of the work style of CPC leaders amid the new situations by promoting new healthy trends and resisting evil trends. To that end, excellent work style in eight aspects must be advocated vigorously: Be diligent and studious and apply what he/she has learned; Truly care for the people and serve the people; Be practical and pursue the effectiveness of work; Work hard and be thrifty; Consider the overall situation and execute every order without fail; Promote democracy and unite as one; Refrain from abusing power and ensure clean governance; Live a decent life and develop healthy interest. As the recognition goes deeper, construction of the work style of the CPC ushered into a new stage. In 2007, the CPC launched a campaign themed on "establishing a new image and making fresh achievements"; In September 2008, the CPC officially initiated a campaign for further learning and practicing the scientific outlook on development, which covered over 3.7 million Party organizations and baptized more than 75 million Party members; In 2009, the CPC organized the activity themed on "Three Services and One Satisfaction"; In 2010, the campaign of working to establish advanced grass-roots Party organizations and to be excellent Party members was carried out nationwide. All these practices and activities resulted in improved work style of Party members and cadres, closer ties between the Party and the people and obviously enhanced credibility of the Party.

In the view of the CPC, the issue of work style has its root in ideology, namely, the outlook on the world, life and values ("Three Outlooks") goes off the right path. After the 18th National Congress of the CPC, the new generation

On April 2, 2014, Party cadres from all parts of the country visited the grave of martyr Jiao Yulu at the Memorial Hall for Comrade Jiao Yulu. Jiao Yulu (1922–1964) was honored as "good Party cadre" and "good public servant for the people".

of the central collective leadership requires all the organizations to check and analyze the root causes of the issue from the perspective of "Three Outlooks" while guiding study and practice of its mass line. The purpose is to thoroughly correct formalism, bureaucracy, hedonism and extravagance, stop Party members from wavering in the Party's ideal and conviction, being weakly aware of his/her purpose, being slack in spirits, seeking fame and fortune or resorting to deceit, and to prevent them from being divorced from the people and reality, being irresponsible and extravagant, or even abusing one's power for personal gains, becoming corruptive and degenerate or behaving in other ways that impair the image of the Party among the people.

After decades of exploration, the CPC has paid growing attention to intensifying construction of its work style through routine systems and to effectively supervising the implementation of the systems. During the education campaign launched recently to execute its mass line, the new generation of the central collective leadership not only highlighted efforts to give better play to the role of democratic activities as an excellent system that the CPC has insisted on for a long time, but also enriched the contents of the system. The *Notice on Doing a Good Job in Launching Democratic Activities in the Party's Mass Line Education Campaign* released by the Central Commission for Discipline Inspection of the CPC, the Organization Department of the CPC Central Committee and the Central Party's Mass Line Education Practice Leading Group in August 2013 pointed out that members of the standing committee of the Political Bureau of the CPC Central Committee must join all the democratic meetings held among the provincial Party leadership where the paired contact sites are located. This was an unprecedented move in rectification. Between September 23-25, 2013, Xi Jinping, General Secretary of the CPC Central Committee, spent four half days attending the democratic meetings under the Party's mass line education campaign held among the members of the standing committee of the CPC Hebei Provincial Committee. Before and after the visit, other members of the standing committee of the Political Bureau of the CPC Central Committee headed for respective sites of paired contact for participation in democratic meetings: Li Keqiang went to Guangxi Zhuang Autonomous Region, Zhang Dejiang to Jiangsu Province, Yu Zhengsheng to Gansu Province, Liu Yunshan to Zhejiang Province, Wang Qishan to Heilongjiang Province, and Zhang Gaoli to Sichuan Province. At the democratic meetings in the provinces or autonomous regions, secretaries of the provincial Party committees conducted self-criticism on behalf of the leadership, and every member of the leadership conducted self-criticism and criticized each other, deeply analyzing causes and proposing measures for rectification and directions of efforts. Members of the standing committee of the Political Bureau of the CPC Central Committee heard the talks and took notes carefully before making comments and offering further guidance. In addition, the Central Committee of the CPC also dispatched 45 central supervision groups in charge of provincial-level officials to various sites of education practice to supervise, inspect and guide activities and execution of systems related to construction of the Party's work style.

Theoretical development and practical exploration in recent years showed that the CPC has paid increasing attention to the construction of its work style, and regarded it as a critical guarantee for addressing ruling tests and alleviating ruling risks under the new historical conditions. Construction of the Party's work style is also being enriched and taken to a path featuring institutions and regularity. This is of great significance for the ruling party to rally public support, coordinate relations of various sides and maintain social harmony and stability.

Strictly Combat Corruption

Corruption is a social and historical phenomenon, a worldwide scourge and an issue with great social concerns. As the only ruling party in China, the CPC has always worked to crack down on corruption inside the Party and regarded it as a major part of its construction.

On one hand, the CPC has kept putting in place systems and mechanisms designed to restrain power, in the hope of checking corruption from the source. In the early years of the New China, the CPC set up a discipline inspection authority and carried out the "Three-anti Campaign and Five-anti Campaign", firmly eliminating corruption and severely punishing a number of corrupt officials including Liu Qingshan and Zhang Zishan to defend the authority of

On April 29, 2014, the Party cadres of Huangshan (Anhui) took classes at the Huangshan Anti-corruption, Clean Governance and Duty Crime Prevention and Warning Education Base.

Party discipline and state laws. After China's reform and opening-up, the CPC further cracked down on corruption while checking corruption at the source through systems. From 1984 to 1988, the Central Committee of the CPC and the State Council respectively released the *Decision on Banning Party and Government Organizations and Cadres from Running Businesses and Enterprises and the Regulations on Further Preventing Party and Government Organizations and Cadres from Running Businesses and Enterprises*. In 1997, the Central Committee of the CPC promulgated the *Numerous Codes for the CPC Members and Cadres to Practice Clean Governance (Trial)*, which was a relatively complete and systematic set of codes of behaviors for clean governance. In February 2010, the said codes that had been implemented on a trial basis for nearly 13 years were finally changed into official ones, which put forward 52 "don'ts" for Party cadres in eight aspects ("don't seek unjustified interests using influence of authority or posts", "don't embark on profit-oriented activities privately", "don't violate against regulations for management and use of public properties and don't exploit public offices for private gains or turn public property into private property", "don't appoint cadres in a way against regulations", "don't seek interests for relatives or co-workers using influence of authority or posts", "don't go in for pomp, keep up with the Joneses, squander public funds or be extravagant", "don't break regulations and intervene in market economic activities for personal gains", "don't be divorced from reality, resort to deceit or impair interests of the mass and the relations between the Party and the mass"), regulated the clean governance behaviors of Party members and cadres and improved corresponding implementation and supervision systems.

On the other hand, the CPC has severely punished violations against discipline within the Party. There are 10 forms of violations. First, violations against political discipline, such as organizing or joining anti-Party assemblies, processions and demonstrations, refusing to execute Party's guidelines, policies or work deployment, joining overseas intelligence agencies or providing them with information. Second, violations against organizational or personnel

On November 26, 2013, the CPC Central Commission for Discipline Inspection held the Open Day activity and invited 17 senior media professionals from EU countries to visit the organizations of the CPC Central Commission for Discipline Inspection to see what the Party has done for building a honest and clean Party and government and carrying out anti-corruption programs since the 18th National Congress of the CPC, and what are the related new arrangements since the Third Plenary Session of the 18th Central Committee of the CPC.

discipline, such as breaking the Party Constitution or intra-Party statutes, going against the principle of democratic centralism or refusing to execute the decisions of the organizations. Third, violations against regulations concerning honesty and self-discipline, such as taking advantage of one's position and power to illegally occupy State, collective or individual properties not run by himself/herself, seek gains for others or waste public properties. Fourth, bribery and corruption practices, such as using one's position and power to plunder, steal or gain public properties by cheating, asking for belongings of others or appropriating public funds for personal use. Fifth, acts against socialist economic orders, such as smuggling, embarking on illegal operations or running businesses against the law. Sixth, violations against financial discipline, such as concealing or holding back any part of State fiscal revenue, depositing public funds in one's own name, or causing loss of the State-owned assets by breaching regulations. Seventh, misconduct and dereliction of duty, such as the abuse of power or neglect of duty in work, losing confidential documents or disclosing State secrets. Eighth, infringement of the rights of Party members or citizens, such as thwarting or suppressing the criticism, prosecution or framing up Party members or citizens, or infringing the rights of Party members or citizens to vote and to stand for election. Ninth, severe violations against socialist morality, such as seeking honor through fraud and deception, refusing to assume the obligation of upbringing and educating one's children or supporting one's parents, or choosing not to save State properties or people's lives or properties under severe threats although he/she is able to do that. Tenth, acts against orders of social administration, such as going whoring, prostitution, drug taking or gathering people to gamble for profits.

Party members involved in the said violations against discipline will be given five kinds of punishments according to the seriousness of cases, namely warning, serious warning, removal from Party posts, probation within the Party, and expulsion from the Party. Warning and serious warning are targeted at slight violations against discipline within the Party. Awarded warning or serious warning, a Party member cannot be promoted within the Party in one year. Removal from Party posts refers to removing a Party member concerned from all the Party posts as elected or appointed, and the Party member removed from Party posts cannot assume posts equivalent to or higher than the former posts within two years. Probation within the Party includes one-year and two-year probation, during which a Party member concerned has no right to participate in voting or elections or stand for election. A Party member who during that time truly rectifies his or her mistake shall have his or her rights as a Party member restored. Party members who refuse to mend their ways shall be expelled from the Party. Expulsion is the ultimate Party disciplinary measure. A Party member awarded the punishment cannot re-join the Party within five years. The leading organizations that seriously violate the Party's discipline shall be reorganized, and the organizations in which all the Party members or most Party members seriously violate the Party's discipline shall be dissolved. All the Party members and organizations must observe the Party's discipline without any individual or organization exceptions. Party Constitution and other statutes of the Party serve as the basis for enforcing the Party discipline, and decisions about detailed punishment must be discussed collectively rather than made by individuals or minorities.

Seriously punishing violations against discipline is a major part of self-management by the CPC, as well as an effective means employed by the CPC to combat corruption and avoid degeneration under market economy. According to the statistics released in 2013, discipline inspection authorities at various levels received 1,306,822 cases of tip-offs and letters, visits and whistle-blowing in 2012, including 866,957 cases of prosecution. Particularly, 171,436 cases involved initially verified clues of violations against laws or discipline, 155,144 cases were registered and 153,704 cases were settled. As a result, 160,718 persons were punished, including 134,464 given Party disciplinary punishment and 38,487 given administrative disciplinary punishment. A total of RMB 7.83 billion of economic loss was saved for the State by handling the cases. In particular, addressing the breach of Party discipline by Bo Xilai, former member of the Political Bureau of the CPC Central Committee and Secretary of the CPC Chongqing Municipal Committee, aroused extensive attention both at home and abroad and demonstrated the resolution of the CPC Central Committee to fight corruption. After the 18th National Congress of the CPC, the CPC Central Committee has continued to improve its work style, defend its discipline and combat corruption. As a result, officials above the provincial level including Li Chuncheng, former vice secretary of the CPC Sichuan Provincial Committee, Zhou Zhenhong, former member of the standing committee of the CPC Guangdong Provincial Committee and minister of the United Front Work Department of CPC Central Committee, Liu Tienan, member of the Party leadership group and vice chairman of the National Development and Reform

Commission, Ni Fake, former vice governor of the People's Government of Anhui Province and member of the Party leading group, Guo Yongxiang, former member of the standing committee of the CPC Sichuan Provincial Committee and vice governor of Sichuan Province, Wang Suyi, Minister of the United Front Work Department of CPC Inner Mongolian Autonomous Region Committee, Li Daqiu, former vice chairman of the CPPCC of Guangxi Zhuang Autonomous Region and chairman of the Federation of Trade Unions as well as Jiang Jiemin, former chairman of the State-owned Assets Supervision and Administration Commission of the State Council, were punished and stepped down.

During the anti-corruption practices, the CPC gradually recognizes that simply relying on strengthening work style and discipline is insufficient to contain and eliminate corruption. Instead, it must make overall deployment and systematic plans to advance work related to anti-corruption in a comprehensive

The Higher People's Court of Shandong Province publicly announced appeal against the case about Bo Xilai's bribery, corruption and abuse of power on October 25, 2013. The picture shows a number of reporters gather in front of the gate of the Higher People's Court of Shandong Province.

manner. Over the past three decades since China's reform and opening-up, the CPC has changed the fight against corruption from "focusing on containment" to "addressing both the symptoms and root causes and exercising comprehensive control" and further to "addressing both the symptoms and root causes, exercising comprehensive control and gradually increasing efforts in removing roots causes" before it proposed the strategic guidelines of "addressing both the symptoms and root causes, exercising comprehensive control and combining punishment with prevention, with the emphasis on prevention". In the 21st century, the strategic guidelines were further improved. In January 2005, the CPC Central Committee released the *Implementation Outline for Establishing and Improving the System for Punishing and Preventing Corruption that Puts Equal Emphasis on Education, Institution and Supervision*, explicitly setting the goal for establishing and improving the system aimed to punish and prevent corruption. That is, after a period of steadfast efforts, the CPC shall "initially establish the long-term mechanism for anti-corruption education, put in place relatively complete regulations for fighting corruption and upholding integrity, basically develop the mechanism for power exercising and supervision, further deepen the reform aimed to prevent corruption at the source, notably improve the work style of both the Party and the government, further contain corruption and see fresh improvements in public satisfaction". To strengthen prevention against corruption, coordinate anti-corruption work by various sides and pool efforts to prevent corruption, the National Bureau of Corruption Prevention was set up in 2007 as pushed by the CPC Central Committee. In May 2008, the CPC Central Committee promulgated the *Work Plan on Establishing and Improving the System for Punishing and Preventing Corruption 2008-2012*, making overall deployment for fighting corruption and upholding integrity with the focus on improving the system for punishing and preventing corruption from multiple aspects including education, institution, supervision, reform, correction of work style and punishment. Following the 18th National Congress of the CPC, the CPC Central Committee further defined the ideas for anti-corruption. In his

On March 9, 2014, Huang Shuxian, deputy secretary of the CPC Central Commission for Discipline Inspection, Minister of Supervision and director general of the National Bureau of Corruption Prevention, said when attending the Second Session of the 12th National People's Congress that, the anti-corruption will be continuously enhanced.

speech delivered at the second plenary meeting of the Central Commission for Discipline Inspection of the CPC, Xi Jinping ordered enhanced restraint and supervision on the use of power. He said, "Power should be contained within a cage of regulations." A disciplinary, prevention and guarantee mechanism should be set up to ensure that people dare not to, are not able to and cannot easily commit corruption.

While making the ideas for anti-corruption more scientific, the CPC keeps expanding the channels for anti-corruption. The Central Commission for Discipline Inspection of the CPC launched a special website to address public tip-offs against the Party members, Party organizations or objects of administrative supervision with violations against the discipline of the Party or the government and to handle the opinions and suggestions concerning the construction of the Party's work style and work related to anti-corruption. The Organization Department of the CPC Central Committee also launched the "12380" website to address reports regarding selecting and appointing cadres by leadership or leaders above the county level as against the *Work Regulations for Selecting and Appointing Party and Government Leaders and Cadres* or relevant regulations. In fact, this is a major means the CPC uses to expand the channel for public involvement in anti-corruption in the Internet-based information age, strengthen collection, analysis and handling of online information about fighting corruption and upholding integrity, and advance progress in the anti-corruption campaign.

Over the past years, the CPC has integrated combating corruption and upholding integrity with socialist economic, political, cultural and social construction, and with every aspect of the Party's construction. By making new achievements in improving the Party's style of work and upholding integrity, the CPC aims to win trust of the people, raise its profile as a ruling party and gain greater public support. With the effective advances in the anti-corruption move, the CPC is expected to enjoy a further consolidated foundation for ruling in the future.